Praise f

In this excellent book, B............. .... .. understanding children, building strong relationships and loving pupils. Based on years of experience working in challenging schools – even the one I went to myself as a kid – he emphasises how vital adult behaviour needs to be in order to get the best out of the pupils. What we see in this book is the power of relationships and how we really must be sophisticated in how we communicate with children in our schools. If you are a new teacher then this book will help you take those first nervous steps into classroom management. If you are an experienced teacher then take a look – you may learn something new.

Dave Whitaker, Director of Learning, Wellspring Academy Trust, former Executive Principal, author of The Kindness Principle, Independent Thinking Associate

Steve properly knows his stuff and communicates it brilliantly. His writing drips with authentic experience from a career in some truly wobbly places. Steve's advice is exactly what you need to upgrade behaviour in your classroom.

Invaluable to early career teachers and experienced practitioners.

Paul Dix, Author of When The Adults Change, Everything Changes

Reading this book gave me hope. Hope to believe that there is a better way to teach and support our children, not least those from broken homes and dysfunctional families. Nelson Mandela suggested that education is the most powerful weapon we can use to change the world. Yet too many of our children are being excluded from lessons and even their own school community every day. If every teacher and every Ofsted inspector were to read this book, and apply the challenges and tools provided in their professional work, I believe we would see outcomes improve and the so-called disadvantage gap close significantly.

Paul Tinsley, Interim Assistant Director of Education, Calderdale

Through visiting thousands of lessons, Steve has a special talent for spotting those moments of interaction between adult and youngsters that are catalysts for relationships breaking down and the inevitable onset of crisis. *That Behaviour Book* looks at those moments, identifies the issues and provides sensible solutions that have proven to work in many schools. This book is an essential read for all adults working with youngsters.

Mark Ayers, Acting Head Teacher, Appleton Academy

'Allowing the teachers to take control of behaviour' is a wonderful summary as Steve looks back and advises on how to teach Wade Booley as his younger self (without taking him around the back of the Portakabin, *Kes*-style). This book helps establish routines and helps build relationships for ECTs and experienced teachers. It is easy to read with a plethora of simple ideas, told in a humerous manner with examples we can all relate to.

The takeaways are a perfect ending to each chapter, but the cherry on the cake are the 'Now Try This' reflective opportunities which allow teachers to make those positive changes. An exceptional read.

Chris Dyson, Deputy CEO, The Create Trust

That BEHAVIOUR BOOK

The Simple Truth About Teaching Children

STEPHEN BAKER

Crown House Publishing Limited
www.crownhouse.co.uk

First published by
Crown House Publishing Ltd
Crown Buildings, Bancyfelin, Carmarthen, Wales, SA33 5ND, UK
www.crownhouse.co.uk

and

Crown House Publishing Company LLC
PO Box 2223
Williston, VT 05495, USA
www.crownhousepublishing.com

British Library of Cataloguing-in-Publication Data

A catalogue entry for this book is available from the British Library.

Print ISBN: 978-178583668-8
Mobi ISBN: 978-178583669-5
ePub ISBN: 978-178583670-1
ePDF ISBN: 978-178583671-8

LCCN 2022948379

Printed and bound in the UK by
CPi, Antony Rowe, Chippenham, Wiltshire

This book is dedicated to the late Andrew Reid

FOREWORD

On our journey through life, we are guaranteed to experience a range of emotions – excitement, tiredness, confusion, happiness and anger. If our school system is to be of worth, we need to understand that children are people too, and strive to lead all the people in our schools with empathy, love and a caring consistency. We must teach them the behaviour we expect. Teachers need to be leaders in their classrooms – and good leaders lead rather than manage.

The pressures on teachers to deliver content and good outcomes is immense. This can only be achieved if we build positive relationships with pupils, and this starts with solid routines. Rita Pierson says in her 2013 TED Talk, 'Kids don't learn from people they don't like.'[1] There is a certain amount of truth in Rita's statement; nevertheless, this book gives adults tried and tested strategies to build trusting relationships in classrooms that are genuine and safe.

In this book, Steve shares the lessons he has learned as a successful teacher of English and drama, as a subject leader and head of year, and as a behaviour and attendance consultant. The strategies are mined from the chalkface of the multitude of schools and classrooms he has visited, mostly in areas of high deprivation.

I have worked with Steve for many years, and I have seen first-hand how his support has developed new teachers and transformed the capacity of established ones, contributing to reduced exclusions, positive inspection reports and a sense that our school is better placed to serve our community.

Whether you are an early career teacher, a senior leader with twenty years' experience or an adult working with young people in a different context, this book is essential reading. Schools simply cannot keep off-rolling pupils. We must learn to lead behaviour in schools, and Steve offers important insights into how we can achieve this.

Mark Ayres, acting head teacher, Appleton Academy, Bradford

---

1 Rita Pierson, Every Kid Needs a Champion [video], *TED* (May 2013). Available at: https://www.ted.com/talks/rita_pierson_every_kid_needs_a_champion?language=en.

ACKNOWLEDGEMENTS

I would like to thank the following:

Emma Tuck, my extraordinary editor, who saw the big picture and nailed the minute detail, all at the same time. The book you are reading is immensely improved by her good works.

David Bowman, Amy Heighton, Beverley Randell and all the team at Crown House Publishing for their unstinting belief and support.

Charlotte Taylor who persuaded me to submit my scribblings to a publisher, and Pran Patel whose encouragement got me over the line.

John Atkinson, Mark Ayres, Paul Dix, Jackie Edwards, Jan Featherstone, Paul Frazer, Jan Linsley, Eileen McCarthy, Paul Wright and the late Andrew Reid, all of whom believed in me and encouraged me to believe in myself at moments when it really mattered.

The teachers I have worked with over the years for their courage, openness and commitment.

Very special thanks go to Sian, Owen and Rhiannon.

CONTENTS

INTRODUCTION

The purpose of this book is to help new teachers manage behaviour more effectively. I would prefer to say 'lead' than 'manage', but we will get to that later. My teaching experience was in secondary schools and you will find that reflected in these pages, but I hope that adults in every setting will find *That Behaviour Book* relevant and helpful. Also, you might not be new to this game; you may be an experienced colleague who feels the need to reset and refresh your approach, and if so, I trust that you too will find what you need here.

I have worked with countless teachers over the last twenty years and have watched them move from despair to delight. As children's behaviour improves, they begin to enjoy the job again, they sleep better and they go home with some energy left for partners, families and other interests. This, after all, is the stuff that adds up to having a life – precious stuff that is crowded out all too easily when worrying about the boys in 9FW fills every corner of your mental space, like expanding foam.

I will mention just one of these teachers, Anka, who had moved to the UK from Eastern Europe with her husband and was training to teach maths in Oldham. Her classes ate her alive at first. After visiting Anka's lesson one morning, I returned at the end of the day to share my feedback, only to find her sitting at her desk, silently weeping. It killed me to see Anka hurting so badly, but I set to work as coach, mentor and sounding board, while she developed the routines, the language and the persona that would put her, benignly, in charge of the room. Several weeks later, the transformation was incredible. Anka had gone from well-meaning doormat to empathetic, effective teacher. She was firmly in charge and enjoyed warm, productive relationships with classes that had once run her ragged. When I moved on some months later, she sent me the most wonderful note: 'I will never have the words to thank you.'

I would like to dedicate this book to Anka and the many others whom it has been my pleasure to support over these last two decades. I hope that, while we spend this time together, I can help you to reflect on your own practice, share some tips you can use straightaway and equip you with strategies that will bring you success. There are 'Takeaways' at the end of each chapter that sum up the key points and also practical 'Now try this' activities to accelerate your progress. I hope that you will enjoy reading the book, that before long you will have your own stories to tell, and that you will enjoy sharing them as much as I have enjoyed sharing mine. Right now, though, let us start at the beginning.

∘ ∘ ∘

The nightmare scenario

You are standing in front of your Year 7 class. All you can see right now are gum-chewing water-bottle jugglers, blame-shifting work avoiders, back-chatting phone addicts, and note-passing gossip fiends. You have been told to expect a senior leadership team (SLT) 'drop-in' observation any time this week.

And you cannot get quiet.

'Listen!' you call, more in hope than expectation. 'Guys! Please!' Your appeals fall on deaf ears. The noise continues. Ewan is struggling to free his bag from Jake's grasp. Tamsir is out of her seat persuading Amal to go out with Elisabeth. David, who usually ignores your pleas for quiet, is today yelling 'Shut up!' at the class in a misguided attempt to help you.

The noise builds, billows and shrieks; this lot are out of control. You may as well try to stop a fast-flowing river. And your mind is racing faster still: 'This is only Year 7! I should be able to control this lot!'

Your chest tightens as your nervous system roars into panic mode. Why won't they listen? When you finally raise your voice at a boy on the nearest table, he turns and with a frown says, 'Chill out, guy!'

Oh, dear …

Evolution has left your body unable to distinguish between an irritating 12-year-old boy and an Earth-bound asteroid about to vaporise you, your house and family. Drowning in adrenaline, your brain screams 'Fight!' or 'Run!'

But you cannot do either of those things. In that millisecond, the general noise, the sneering boy, the threat of imminent SLT observation, your harrowing sense of inadequacy and your own biology have you rooted to the spot. You try to think … but you may as well try to sprint in lead boots.

It is your move.

What you do will depend on your answer to several questions. What do you believe about behaviour and about young people? What is your purpose as a teacher? How should young people be disciplined? Are you confident in your own ability? Are you in a good place emotionally?

o o o

After seventeen years of teaching, this kind of experience is a vivid if not particularly cherished memory for me. It is still the daily waking nightmare for many teachers, and the purpose of this book is to help the adults who read it to put themselves back in charge of behaviour.

Of course, there are those who seek to put teachers back in charge by giving them big sticks to wield. They set up rigid systems that lead to pupils being sent out, detained, isolated and, ultimately, excluded over issues that could have been sorted with a little empathy and good grace on the part of the adults. In the face of this inflexibility, some children simply vote with their feet.

This book assumes that we need to teach *all* the children in our catchment area, that children need our help the most when we may feel they deserve it the least, and that with consistent adult behaviour based on values, beliefs and principles, we can lead behaviour in an entirely new direction.

My idealism was not fully formed when I started out, by the way. It has been informed by experience and has grown stronger over the years. I taught my first lesson as a trainee teacher in a grim Portakabin, squatting in the yard of a West Yorkshire comprehensive. For some reason, I thought I would try to be gruff but fair. Ha! After five minutes, I found myself in a 'Yes-you-bloomin'-will/No-I-bloomin'-won't' confrontation with a lad called Wade Booley. In that moment, it felt like a matter of life and death; me or him. Wade was a few inches taller than me so I cannot say we were nose to nose; more nose to Adam's apple. I do not remember what I told him to do, just that he point-blank refused to do it. He stood his ground, smirking at my laughable attempt to get my own way, while my heart thumped like a jackhammer.

You hear people say, 'my blood boiled'; well, it felt like that. Fight or flight? Flock or freeze? Funny how all those words start with an 'F', like some others I wanted to use. I was stuck in a hellish cul-de-sac and the only available gear was reverse. This was my first climb-down and my most painful. I know it was painful because, and I am deeply ashamed to admit this, I awoke next morning utterly horrified, having dreamt of thumping the poor boy.

At least I only dreamed of doing it. The teacher whose class I was standing in front of (I will not say 'teaching') told me that he regretted the passing of the good old days when 'we could take them behind the Portakabin and give them a good hiding'. Who said *Kes* was exaggerated?

The subject tutors on my PGCE course taught me little about teaching English and less about behaviour. We were told to be keen and smiley and the kids would love us. There is a grain of truth in that, of course, but enthusiasm will only get you so far. Behaviour leadership is all about trust. How was Wade Booley ever going to trust me on day one? Like all young people, he will have been craving the company of relaxed, empathetic and authoritative adults, and I clearly did not fit the bill. Thirty-seven years later, I can laugh about all this, and write in this book the advice I would have given to my younger self.

In a nutshell, behaviour improves when teachers invest in relationships, establish robust routines and speak calmly to children. It improves when they explicitly teach the behaviour they want to see (just as they teach maths, phonics or geography), when they teach it by means of their own good example and when they teach it by highlighting good behaviour when they see it. Oh, and by the way, in order to safeguard the privacy of pupils, I have changed their names.

I hope you will find this book helpful.

Chapter 1

VALUES

The first question to ask yourself is, what do you believe about children and behaviour? How your classes behave will depend to some extent on how *you* behave, and that will depend on your mindset. This chapter sets out the values, beliefs and principles that I believe are essential if we are to achieve positive and productive relationships with young people in classrooms and around school.

What is your mission?

Why are you doing this job? I drifted into teaching because I wanted to be an actor. I told the Fellow in Theatre at Bradford University of my ambition to act and, by way of letting me down gently, he suggested a postgraduate drama teaching qualification at Bretton Hall (home of the wonderful Yorkshire Sculpture Park), and then? Well, 'See what happens ...' Plenty of acting careers were launched at Bretton but, sadly, mine was not among them. Instead, I stayed the course and, hey presto, I stumbled on a career that became my passion.

Many secondary teachers have told me that they chose teaching because they did not know what else to do with their degree, and there is no shame in that. But teaching is a very demanding job, so you will need a sense of mission to sustain you; a higher purpose that goes above and beyond the mere delivery of facts to young minds. You might think this advice is a little obvious, but I have met countless teachers who have lost that sense of mission. Ground down by workload, the relentless nature of the school timetable and the pressure for results, they have ended up just getting through the week, which becomes just getting through the day and just getting through the hour. You need to hang on to your idealism at all costs, as it will sustain you.

Your content or your audience?

New teachers face some sobering experiences. You may enter the class-room proudly bearing aloft the precious gift of Mozart, maths or modern languages … and collide with a brick wall of apathy. You may be left feeling angry, hurt and even a little insecure – were you right to devote your life to a subject that leaves these youngsters so stubbornly unmoved? Some staff never get over that sense of rejection. Accepting that you are there to educate the person as well as teach your subject is vital.

I have been known to announce to a roomful of teachers during a behaviour training day, 'We are now going to do some role play,' and you would think I had handed them an anthrax sandwich. If looks could kill, I would be dead meat. But I am not a sadist by nature and so I let them off. 'Only kidding!' I tell them. 'But hang on to that feeling. Announcing your favourite topic can cause your pupils the very same panic that you are feeling right now.'

Some of these adults lack empathy; they treat the prospect of role play as if it were botulism, but they cannot imagine why their pupils recoil in fear from fractions or French verbs. Children are not a different species, so why should we expect them to respond differently? Seeing the classroom situation from your learners' point of view is a vital skill. For some teachers, children are nothing more than little problems to be managed, but this prevents them from ever engaging with children and enjoying their company. If you can see that these young humans have a valid take on the world, you will be ahead of the game.

You have no control over the lives your pupils have led, the families who have raised them or their previous experiences of the subject you are attempting to teach, but all these factors will affect their readiness to engage with you. Being passionate about Spanish is a wonderful thing, but what will you do if your classes show no interest in languages whatsoever? Where will you start? How much empathy can you muster for those who reject everything you hold dear?

I ask these questions to point you towards the bigger picture. Great teachers find common ground with their pupils, and they do it because they know that they are educators in the broadest sense first, and their subject content is secondary to that. As Mark Finnis likes to put it, 'connect before content'.[1]

Another challenge to your confidence is the child's developing brain. Teenagers are designed to frustrate adults. They crave risk-taking and abhor responsibility. Everything we believe in seems pointless to them, and everything they obsess about can seem entirely trivial to us. This can fuel a lack of respect which destroys any chance of connection. We must be generous, leave our egos at the door and be prepared to meet the children where they are now, not where we would like them to be.

The staffroom

The staffroom can go two ways. It can be a welcoming oasis of brilliant ideas and mutual support, or it can be a dark, poisonous well. The devil has all the best tunes when it comes to the staffroom. Everybody likes a good moan, and there are often one or two staff who like to hold court, subjecting anyone within earshot to their negativity. I hear, with depressing regularity, pupils sorted into the 'good kids' and the 'bad kids', and I have concluded that good kids are those who will put up with dull lessons without complaint. As for the bad kids, well, whatever their circumstances, they seem to be fair game. I get told that so-and-so is a 'cocky little shite', that another child is 'a drama queen' and that is not the worst of it.

In my experience, the pupils who come in for this kind of abuse when their backs are turned have experienced literacy problems, broken homes, poor housing, domestic abuse, childhood trauma and endless other issues. It is simplistic and just plain wrong to label them 'bad'. This is what happens when teachers lose sight of the bigger picture and all sense of mission. They are taking young people as they are, which only makes them worse, when we should be taking them as they could be. It is our job to see the potential in every child, not to write them off before they get started.

---

1   Mark Finnis, *Restorative Practice* (Carmarthen: Independent Thinking Press, 2021), p. 7.

These staff like nothing better than a new recruit, so beware the staffroom cynics who would entice you into their web of despair. As Haim Ginott famously concluded in his book, *Teacher and Child*:

> I have come to a frightening conclusion. I am the decisive element in the classroom. It is my personal approach that creates the climate. It is my daily mood that makes the weather. As a teacher I possess tremendous power to make a child's life miserable or joyous. I can be a tool of torture or an instrument of inspiration. I can humiliate or humor, hurt or heal. In all situations it is my response that decides whether a crisis will be escalated or de-escalated, and a child humanized or de-humanized.[2]

Your job as a teacher is to help young people build their futures, to assist them to thrive and to achieve their potential. You may be the first reliable, caring adult a child meets. What a responsibility! And the thing about children is, as any parent will tell you, they do not fall over themselves to thank you for the sacrifices you make: the late-night marking you do, the play rehearsals you put on, the break times you give up supervising their downtime, the social life that suffers while you overhaul that dated curriculum you inherited. Teaching is a wonderfully rewarding occupation, but it is also a very stressful one, and without a strong sense of moral purpose you can easily become lost.

Taking responsibility

You are responsible for behaviour in your lessons. There, I have said it. When we describe 'bad behaviour' in the classroom, we are talking about pupils *not engaged in learning*. You are responsible for engaging your pupils in learning, ergo you are responsible for behaviour. QED. This idea appals some staff. 'How can you blame me for what Kerry-Jo, Dylan and Jake are doing?' they cry, but, in fact, it is a liberating thought. If behaviour was solely the pupils' responsibility, you would be powerless, but you are not. Your pupils may bring the weather, but you set the climate. They might stomp into the room after a falling out in the yard at break time, but you create the space they stomp into. With clear routines, explicit positive

---

2   Haim G. Ginott, *Teacher and Child: A Book for Parents and Teachers* (New York: Macmillan, 1972), p. 15.

expectations and a genuine welcome, you can make things better; you can create a climate that will vastly improve the behaviour of the many and make the determined poor behaviour of the few far easier to deal with.

When I was contemplating teaching as a career, I was lucky to know a wonderful man called Andrew Reid. A gentler soul was never born. Andrew was a school inspector, a Methodist local preacher and a former primary head teacher. Among all the advice he gave me, one sentence stands out: 'Your pupils must know that *Mr Baker cares*.' Andrew's life was tragically cut short by Hodgkin's disease, but his words have lived long in my memory.

Some staff send pupils out all the time. 'Go and talk to someone who's paid more,' they say. 'I'm here to teach.' One of the many things that is wrong with this approach is that it is self-defeating. If you send a pupil to see a member of pastoral staff with the attitude of 'bring this child back when it's fixed', they may develop a decent relationship and perhaps even a strong attachment to your pastoral colleague, but none of this will benefit you. Next lesson, you will be back at square one.

When pupils get it wrong, you really can do your own repair and rebuild work, and you will benefit from doing it. Holding restorative conversations with pupils is essential to building trusting relationships. Schools have found that allowing staff to send pupils out causes more problems than it solves. The corridors fill up, those sent out go missing, on-call staff are overwhelmed and on-site resources are pushed to breaking point. Of course, now and again, something serious occurs in a classroom and, for safety's sake, a pupil needs to be exited from a room, but that is rare. I frequently hear from on-call staff who have been summoned because a child will not remove their coat; not exactly a situation endangering the survival of the species. The teacher could simply have logged the refusal, informed the child that there would be a consequence, which they would find out about later, and carried on teaching. This would benefit everyone concerned, and it would exemplify 'taking responsibility for behaviour'.

You do not need to refer everything up or send pupils out whenever they cross you. Instead of making the child pay, help the child to *learn*. You do not need revenge, you simply need to support the child to reflect on their behaviour. And you may not need an hour of their time. If they engage in discussion with you and see a way to doing better next time, five minutes or even two might be enough.

At this early stage, you need to know that I have, as they say, been on a journey. During my first year of teaching, I attempted to teach a boy called Rob. He was a classic naughty schoolboy, not a big hitter by any stretch of the imagination. His forte was the simple stuff: turning around, chatting, laughing. Nothing you would call serious, but for some reason Rob *really* got under my skin. I would frequently lose my rag and march him up to an office where Terry, the deputy head, sat glowering over his paperwork. Over and over this happened, lesson after lesson. I can only imagine Terry's joy, God rest his soul, as he heard my angry footsteps on the stairs, day after day. Did I think he owned a magic wand? Later, I would see Rob around school, still in possession of all four limbs, and I would moan to anyone who would listen: 'What's Terry done, eh? Just had a *chat* with him, I suppose?' What did I expect Terry to do? Tie Rob to a stake and burn him? Pull out his eyes and play swingball with them?

Looking back, I was blinkered. I did not see my classroom within any kind of bigger picture, such as the efforts of society to educate its young or even the life chances of young Rob, let alone a developing relationship in which I had a big say. Mine was just a gut-level 'him or me' response that Wade Booley would have recognised. I fess up to all this because I want you to know that the stuff that I bang on about in this book *can be learned*.

Behaviour is a form of communication

Focusing purely on behaviour does not make much sense, if you think about it. The way we behave is a symptom of how we feel at any given moment. Take me to a record store and I will behave very differently than if I am forced to spend time at a craft fair. (I have massive respect for people who embroider and crochet, by the way; it's just not my thing.) How we behave is a function of how loved and valued we feel at any given moment, plus how clear we are about what is expected of us. If I am told in advance that we need to visit a craft fair to find a present for our niece, I will be more cooperative than if I am suddenly dragged in there without warning.

Children are no different. Their behaviour is a function of how they are feeling, how clear expectations have been made and how well routines are established. Inappropriate behaviour tells us there is an unmet need somewhere. If we can change those feelings, we can change the behaviour. The 'nightmare scenario' class are telling you something. The message might be:

- We don't know you, so we don't trust you.

- We have had supply teachers for ages, so we feel neglected and we want revenge.

- You don't look like you want to be here, so we will give you a reason to be miserable.

- You haven't set a routine, so we aren't following one.

- The lesson is boring/irrelevant.

- The lesson is so hard that we have given up.

- The lesson is so easy that we feel disrespected.

- We have been told we are bottom set, that we are the bad kids, so we may as well act accordingly.

Most of these factors are within your control. You cannot do anything about what happened in the past, but what happens from now on is your business. So drip by drip, week by week, you can make a difference.

Another great piece of advice I was given about teaching came from my tutor John Atkinson at Bretton Hall in the mid-1980s: 'Working with young people is a privilege. The price you pay for that privilege is some very upsetting experiences.'

The access we have to young minds – our ability to shape futures – is a rare thing. Our classes need to see us enjoying that privilege. So, if you want to know what works with the tough classes, what breaks down the concrete walls that some young people erect around themselves, this is the answer: show them how much you enjoy the privilege of being with them. Act like you simply could not be taken away from this class, even if Tom Hardy or Anne Hathaway or ___ (insert your own object of desire) were at the classroom door holding tickets for a holiday in Mustique that no one would ever know about and begging you to join them. Your answer to this daydream has to be 'No! Go away, Tom! I want to be here with these kids!'

It must genuinely seem as if there is nowhere on this Earth you would rather be than with this ragtag Year 8 group at this moment. Teaching algebra to silly, lazy, ill-mannered teenagers really must appear to be a much more exciting prospect than sun, sea and the creature of your dreams. That does not mean you need to behave like a gushing fool; you simply need to look like you want to be there.

The growth mindset

The German poet Goethe once wrote, 'When we take people ... merely as they are, we make them worse; when we treat them as if they were what they should be, we improve them as far as they can be improved.'[3]

When I read aloud the John Cooper Clarke poem 'I Wanna Be Yours' to my Year 9 English class at Stocksbridge High School in the late 1990s, I had absolutely no idea that one of my pupils, Alex Turner, would go on to become the lead singer and songwriter of the Arctic Monkeys or that the quiet and reserved Matt Helders would explode into rock superstardom with him. I remember very clearly a parents' evening when Mrs Turner sat in front of me, utterly dejected by my colleagues' comments about her son. 'Don't worry, Mrs Turner,' I said. 'I'm sure Alex is going to turn out OK.'

It would have been easy to write off Alex as a terminally laid-back underachiever. Instead, I focused on the creative original mind that was developing in front of me. I have since been rewarded by seeing his career go global and having the 'Coolest Man on the Planet', as voted by the *New Musical Express* in 2005, call me 'sir' in an email.

This focus on what pupils *might be* and not what they currently *are* was popularised by American psychologist Carol Dweck.[4] Some want to debunk the growth mindset theory because dissection of the human brain has failed to identify the relevant machinery, but at a common-sense level it makes sense. Pupils are learning to behave, just as they are learning French or mathematics. Those who fail in school do not always fail in life. There are enough self-made multi-millionaires in possession of damning school

---

3   Johann Wolfgang von Goethe, *Wilhelm Meister's Apprenticeship and Travels. Translated from the German of Goethe by Thomas Carlyle*, vol. 2 (London: Chapman and Hall, 1824 [1796]), Book VIII, Chapter IV, p. 93.

4   Carol S. Dweck, *Mindset: The New Psychology of Success* (New York: Ballantine, 2013).

reports to make that point irrefutable. Always keep in mind the pleasant and successful adult who is struggling to get out of even the most irritating child. And this growth mindset applies to you too. To the self-lacerating statement, 'My classes don't behave well', you can add the word 'yet'. 'My classes don't behave well *yet*' is a very different statement. With determination and the right support you will get there. You are developing just as much as your pupils.

We don't have to like them

No, we just have to love them. Some years ago, I was lucky enough to attend a conference on behaviour at the Oval cricket ground in London. One of the contributors was a young assistant head teacher from a secondary school in North London. She began her presentation by describing the catchment area and the social problems that came with it. She described pupil motivation and behaviour as it had once been and the tremendous change that had been achieved in recent years. Her PowerPoint presentation had me wiping tears from my eyes. Very simply, we saw pairs of pictures: the same pupils photographed in Year 7 and Year 11. Each picture bore a number – the pupil's predicted attainment in Year 7 on the first one and their actual attainment upon leaving at the end of Year 11 on the second, which in every case way exceeded expectation. It was stunning. Don't tell anyone, but I am welling up now just thinking about it, several years later.

At the end of her presentation, this young assistant head took questions. A deputy head from the West Midlands put up his hand and someone brought him the microphone: 'You've obviously achieved great things, but many of the actions you've taken are things that many schools do. Can you put your finger on what has really made the difference?' Her answer was simple: 'We love our kids.'

Love in this context means a whole load of things. It means providing a safe and calm environment, remaining curious, creating boundaries, taking pupils not as they are but as they could be, showing them personal warmth, expecting great things from them and accepting nothing but their best. If there is one quality that I wish I could inject into the bloodstream of many teachers, it is empathy. If you can see every lesson and every interaction from the young person's point of view, you will be on the right track because what you say and do will have some meaning to them.

Great, enjoyable lessons

When I worked for Wakefield local authority, I had the privilege of supporting Hemsworth Arts and Community College in its attempts to increase attendance. The head teacher, Dave Sharp, was an inspirational figure; a man who, like Mr Chips, had worked his way up from classroom teacher to become head teacher in the same school. He was a local man with a strong Yorkshire accent – and his slogan for efficient teaching was wonderfully simple: 'Gerrem in, gerrem on wi' it, an' gerrem aht!'

I was sitting among his staff at the start of a training day, and Mr Sharp's introduction was a straightforward challenge to his staff: 'Is your lesson worth turning up for?' He had the generosity of spirit to describe a lesson of his own the previous week that had not gone well; in this way, he led from the front. No one was left in any doubt: if we want young people to respect us and engage with education, the first thing we must get right is the quality of teaching. There is simply no substitute for preparing and teaching great lessons, and if behaviour in one of your classes is not great, the first thing to do is to examine what you are teaching and how.

I was about to carry out a lesson visit with a head of maths who was teaching his Year 9s. As we neared the classroom, I asked him what the lesson would be about. He pulled a face and sighed heavily. 'Ratios,' he said, almost despairingly. If he was not looking forward to it, how could his pupils possibly be enthused? If we are bored, then they will be too.

Early in my career, I fell into the trap of telling a class, 'If your behaviour were better, we could do all *sorts* of interesting things!' Since they would not stop talking and paid little attention to my commands, I stuck to a safety-first curriculum, welding bums to seats and noses to textbooks. This set off a vicious circle of boredom, frustration and poor behaviour. Then, one day, inspired by the Theatre in Education team at the Sheffield Crucible, I took a risk, did something different (a dance lesson, would you believe) and, to my astonishment, behaviour improved. I had nothing to lose and everything to gain by ringing the changes and letting go a little.

A head teacher once told me that he could not accept the Every Child Matters agenda because of the requirement that pupils should 'enjoy' and 'achieve'. He said, 'Some subject material is just a grind – it has to be learned and there's no way around that.' Well, yes, the poem or the thermal dynamics may potentially be a grind, but if that grind is ground in the company of a personable, empathetic adult, then there will be enough enjoyment to go around.

Think about the most recent continuing professional development (CPD) you attended. Did the trainer seem engaged and pleased to be there? Did you feel like you were learning? If the answer to both questions is yes, then you probably enjoyed the training. If, on the other hand, you did not think you were learning, then you will almost certainly have switched off. Your mind will have wandered, and as you sank ever lower into your chair, the temptation to check your email or text a friend will have become overwhelming. Teaching imaginative, well-planned lessons will not neutralise the weaponry of the hardened warrior who has arrived at your lesson with the sole intention of trashing it, but it will keep many with you who might otherwise go the other way. I have set out a few questions to ask about your own lessons in Appendix 6.

Staying grounded

Every now and then a penny drops and I learn a lesson. A clunking great penny dropped loud and hard in a classroom one lunchtime, early in my teaching career – but before I describe this embarrassing scene, I need to explain something. I was not the most mature 24-year-old who ever entered the profession. Not that I was immature exactly, but I had been raised in a family who bonded over banter, and so, as a teacher who wanted to be friendly and knew only one way to make friends, I made jokes. It was the only club in my bag. I made *a lot* of jokes.

I could usually be found in the staffroom at lunchtime, doing the *Guardian* quick crossword with my pal, Ian, who taught geography, but for some reason that day I was in a classroom. Perhaps I was looking for someone, I don't know. Anyway, there were a few kids dotted around; I think they were Year 9s, so maybe 13 or 14 years old. One of the girls was eating a bag of crisps, and I was hungry, so I sidled up with a big smile, thinking I was being hilarious, and made to pinch a crisp, saying, 'Come on, then, pay your teacher tax!'

The girl very kindly allowed me to take a crisp, but then she did me a much bigger favour. She looked me straight in the eye and said, 'Why didn't you just *ask* for one?' My immediate reaction was to feel a complete and utter knob. After all, I had just acted like one. I smiled weakly and slunk away, saying, 'Yes, of course. You're right. I will next time. Thanks.' I was painfully embarrassed but thankful too; I had just been taught a profound lesson. There had been no need to make a joke of it, and I did not need to refer to our power relationship, even in a humorous way. This schoolgirl was a person, and she was perfectly ready to see me as a person. I could have simply asked for a crisp, one human being to another.

By the same token, there was a member of the SLT at the school who, when answering the staffroom door to children, would rear up to her full height, flutter her eyelids, raise her eyebrows, lean slowly forwards and say, 'Ye-es?' Informed by the crisp incident, I used to see this performance and wonder why she did not just open the flipping door, like she would to any adult. There was no need to remind the child of the power imbalance between them. This is what being grounded means. Your role gives you a certain authority within a power structure in the school; you do not need to keep beating pupils over the head with this fact. Be yourself.

Of course, being yourself requires self-knowledge. You need to know who you are and what you are giving. The crisp business told me that issues from my own childhood required attention; the kids in my care needed a stable adult, not the office clown. Once you know who you are, you will know what you are bringing to the party. What can you teach children about life, other than your subject? What are your values? What do you believe about the potential for human beings to lead purposeful, satisfying lives? And how we can help each other do that?

Children are people

I hope a 'lightbulb moment' still works as an analogy for a sudden moment of insight. In this age of low-energy light bulbs, a lightbulb moment may soon probably be redefined as the slow dawning of realisation. Anyway, I digress; the lightbulb moment I want to tell you about happened inside the brain of one George Lyward, founder of Finchden Manor, a school for emotionally disturbed boys in Kent from the 1950s to 1970s. Lyward had a gift for enabling boys to take control of their behaviour and to set themselves on the path to success. His pupils included Tom Robinson, who went on to rock stardom, writing 'Glad To Be Gay', among other hits, and then a career in radio journalism. Lyward's flash of insight was so simple that it might seem almost banal, but if you think of it in the right way, it is extraordinarily powerful: children are people. Yes, that is it. A truly great therapeutic and educational career followed from this simple perception. Children are not a separate species; they are simply inexperienced *people*.

I was reminded of this one summer's day on supply at a school in South Yorkshire. Eighty or so Year 11 pupils had finished their maths exam, and with only forty minutes left until lunch, they were herded into a large classroom with a screen at one end. The staff said they could watch last year's James Bond film to relax until the bell. What do you think these 16-year-olds did? Of course, they began talking. They had just spent two hours in silence doing a vital examination; now, they were being shown a film that anyone with the slightest inclination to watch would have seen long ago.

And what do you think the staff did? They went ballistic! The film was stopped, a teacher stood up and berated Year 11 for their ingratitude, and then the film was restarted. And so did the chatter. The brake was applied once more while the head of year was found, and he was wheeled out to lambast the ungrateful horde. And for what? For taking the opportunity to do what any adult would have done in that situation – talk to their peers who had just experienced the same exam. If the adults had realised that children (and, for heaven's sake, these were 16-year-olds – old enough to smoke, get married with parental permission and fight for their country) are people, they would not have behaved as they did.

There is a message here for school leaders about the relationship between the adults and the young people. Leadership from the top needs to model empathy on the basis that pupils are people and will behave like (young) people do. It did not take a genius to see this situation for what it was.

We are an event in *their* lives

I can still remember most of the names of my first Year 10 drama class in 1986. And that is not because they gave me a nice time. I would spend most of my week dreading the hours I was forced to share with Neil B and Paul F. They had no respect for me and even less interest in the subject. I saw them as a blight on my week; a nasty event to be weathered and endured. Their unique perspective on the world did not occur to me. I was feeling sorry for myself and not empathising.

Instead of being hurt and angry, instead of resenting their intrusion into my world, I should have seen myself as an event in *their* lives. I would have reflected on my own behaviour, and I would have begun to understand theirs. In my early to mid-twenties, I failed to summon up the necessary distance from which I could have been the calm, supportive adult. I had been too keen to be their friend, and when they cut up rough, I was too quick to take things personally. I did not (yet) understand how deeply I needed to respect them, if they were ever going to respect me.

The pupils in our care are growing, making mistakes, finding their feet, trying on attitudes and behaviours for size, undergoing the rewiring of the brain that accompanies adolescence, dealing with traumatic experiences, and suffering neglect and other forms of abuse. Is it any wonder that their behaviour sometimes goes awry? Paul Dix nails the necessary mindset in *After the Adults Change*: 'calm adult helping distressed child'.[5] And that is true whether that distressed child is a silent 5-year-old in the foetal position under a table or a 14-year-old bouncing off the corridor walls.

If we truly respect young people, we will not seem afraid. Successful teachers appear pleased to see pupils on the corridor and do not quicken their step when they spot that group of tall Year 11 pupils loitering ahead. When young people sense they are being judged, that the adult has decided they are a 'badass', it is only natural for them to decide, 'I may as well *be* a

---

5   Paul Dix, *After the Adults Change: Achievable Behaviour Nirvana* (Carmarthen: Independent Thinking Press, 2021), p. 21.

badass.' If you can be seen to enjoy the company of young people, to spend a moment or two with them at break, rather than diving into the staffroom and slamming the door gratefully behind you, you will find the love coming back in your direction. And if you do not enjoy the company of children, well, that begs the question. Maybe another career would be a smart move.

'Yes,' I hear you say. 'I believe all that stuff and I do all of those things – and still my pupils misbehave. They won't stop talking, they shout out, they answer back and break every little rule about uniform, equipment and the rest of it.'

OK, I hear you. That is what the rest of this book is about.

Takeaways

- We do not need to like our pupils; we just need to love them.

- All behaviour is a form of communication.

- Instead of making children pay, we need to help them learn.

- Working with young people is a privilege; never value your content more than your audience.

NOW TRY THIS:

Create a survey of your pupils. What is it like to be a pupil of yours? There is a model survey in Appendix 2, but feel free to create your own. Survey Monkey is a quick, free and convenient way to do it. Reflect on the answers you get.

Chapter 2

RESPONDING TO INAPPROPRIATE BEHAVIOUR

Maybe you picked up this book because you are in crisis with your own version of Rob, or worse. You are fretting about this and possibly even losing sleep. The 'nightmare scenario' I described in the introduction to this book is your daily reality, and you want to know what the heck to do. Recently, I bought a new microwave oven. I fought my way through twenty-four pages of the manual, enduring safety advice and helpful tips, learning that I shouldn't operate it outdoors or in a burning building and that I shouldn't use it to dry off a wet dog. Eventually, buried in small print on page 25, was how to turn the darned thing on! I do not want to do that to you, so I am placing this chapter here.

Firstly, stay calm, or at least *act* calm. Pupils must not be able to see that their behaviour can trigger your emotions. If you are calm, you are trustworthy. Breathe slowly and deeply. Your fight-or-flight systems will be lighting up and leading you in the wrong direction, unless you take charge of your breathing to put yourself back in control when reason, logic and scripts have gone out of the window. (We will look at some useful micro-scripts later on in this chapter.) Breathe in slowly for three, hold it for a count of four and breathe out for five. In through the nose and out through the mouth. I have used this technique myself and helped close family members through crises using it, and I can tell you that it works.

It will help you to maintain rational thought and give you time to consider your next step. Otherwise, your emotions will hijack you and you will set off your nuke way too early, something like, 'You! Get out! Go and see the head teacher!' You will be told where to get off, and you will look weak.

It is important to recognise that we cannot control children. It would be great if they came with a remote control that we could pick up and operate, but sadly that is not the case. Great behaviour management is often confused with magic because good teachers appear to make pupils behave without *making* them do anything. Understanding the limits of your naked power is the first step in this direction. We cannot actually *make* them. Grasp this, and then you can relax a little bit. If they do not slavishly follow your commands on day one, that does not mean you are somehow inadequate; it simply means there is a distance to go in establishing routines, giving and receiving respect, investing in relationships and so on. Right now, in this second, you cannot win so don't even try. Play a long game. For today, in the teeth of the nightmare scenario, just staying calm is a victory.

Look calm

At this stage, looking calm is almost certainly an act. But act you must. Take control of your breathing and slow it down. Stand up straight. If you are hunched over or twisted this speaks of inner turmoil, but if you can stand up straight, you will be on your way to exercising some benign natural authority. Now, make sure you are standing still. The film director Clint Eastwood has been known to give the following direction to his actors: 'Don't just do something, stand there!'[1]

Less is more. People who command authority do not fidget. Choose a strong position in the classroom and plant your feet. From time to time, you will need to tour the room, of course, but right now find a strong position, usually at the front and centre, and stay there. Shifting feet look weak, so stand still and this will reinforce the sense that you are a calm, competent adult, comfortable with being in charge. Perhaps only some, or even none, of that feels true right now, but it is the impression you give that matters. Be aware of what your hands are doing. Are you fiddling with your hair, or with loose change in your pocket, or are you wringing your hands? If so, stop.

Carrying out a 'behaviour walk' in a Yorkshire secondary school, I wandered into a classroom and found Jill, a young English teacher, who was struggling with her Year 10 class. Unfortunately, she had reached a moment of crisis and, taking my entry as an opportunity to escape, fled the room. I was left standing in front of a class I had not seen before. There was total silence, not because I had a magic wand but because it was obvious to the class that their behaviour had driven away their teacher, and they were a

---

1   Quoted in Gerald Lubenow, Rebel In My Soul, *Newsweek* (22 July 1985), p. 54.

little shocked. They must have wondered what I was going to say. Resisting the temptation to express anger on Jill's behalf, I said nothing. I looked around the room. I gave some sparing eye contact. I walked down the aisle and back again. It was at least a minute before I spoke.

A few days later, on my next visit to the school, a boy from the class approached me in the corridor: 'Eh up, it's James Bond, innit!' Now, believe me, although I wish it were otherwise, I bear no similarity to any actor who has ever played 007. However, my moment of saying and doing nothing, of remaining calm when I might have been tempted to scream accusations, had given me status in the eyes of that class.

Is it really all of them?

I was sitting in a senior leader's office the other day in a school where I do some consultancy work. I had been left alone to type up lesson visits that I had made that week. One of the assistant head teachers had left her radio in the office and switched on. Not the 'Top 40' kind of radio, you understand. No, this radio was of the 'Crisis kicking off, anyone available please?' variety. Busying myself with my report, I also kept one ear open.

> 1.17pm:
>
> 'On-call to C13 please, it's Dominic. Over.'
>
> 'Roger that. Jenny speaking. What's he done now? Over.'
>
> 'His usual … Over.'
>
> 'Oh heck. How's Hyacinth? Over.'
>
> 'She's in Carol's office with Rescue Remedy and a Rich Tea. Over.'
>
> 1.53pm:
>
> 'On-call please! Room D6. It's Mr Benning. He says it's all of them. Over.'

It's all of them. Not one or two. Not several. Not even a working majority. No, it's all of them. It's something I often hear, but I never, ever see.

The only example I have come across of an entire class getting involved in bad behaviour was back at Ilford County High School in 1976. Our desks were the old-fashioned wooden type with a hinged lid, which you could bang to great effect, and an ink well, which even then was a relic from a bygone era. The desks were decorated in the same way that remote French caves are, with prehistoric gouges and crevices scored by our predecessors over the previous, well, 100 years seemed about right. The surface of these desks resembled nothing so much as Keith Richards' face.

One day, our form teacher made a howling tactical error. He told us that we would be getting new desks, which were going to be delivered the following day. What did we do that lunchtime? Let me just say that we warmed to our task. An orgy of destruction; every boy in the form pounding those desks to bits. A blistering hail of cynical violence unseen anywhere else, except perhaps between Leeds United and Chelsea in the 1970 FA Cup Final. Our version of kicking the opposition was to destroy their furniture. God, we had fun! By 12.55pm there was nothing but splinters, iron and dust.

As we took in the sight of our newly emptied room, it began to dawn on us that punishment might be coming our way and so the principle of 'safety in numbers' applied. Every boy was made to smash something. It was like dipping your hands in Caesar's blood.

Next morning, the head made his one and only visit to our form room in five years in order to remonstrate with such passion that we thought he might burst into tears. If we had seen him more often, we might have cared.

But this is the only time I have ever known a *whole class* behave badly.

When your classroom resembles a cross between a fairground and a secure facility, it is only ever a few pupils who are running the show. They interrupt you, which gives other pupils the opportunity to innocently start talking as the lesson grinds to a halt. They side-track you into stupid disputes, prolonging the interruption. They get up and annoy other people, which provokes those who otherwise were not involved into minor acts of an antisocial nature. And so on.

Basically, there are three types of child in that scenario:

- Kid A: Deliberately making trouble and apparently not fearing any consequences.

- Kid B: Getting distracted and talking to her friends about anything but the lesson.

- Kid C: Trying heroically to concentrate on his work, blotting out the chaos that whirls around his ears.

In most classes you will have a small number of A's, a tiny number of C's and the vast majority will be B's. If you can learn to assert your values, routines and consequences, you will have those B's with you quite soon.

If it ever feels like it's all of them, there is one thing you can do and that is get a second opinion. Ask a colleague you can trust to pop in for ten minutes when you next have this class. They will almost certainly see things you have not.

Anger makes us stupid

I vividly remember back in 1993, when I was lucky enough to attend one of his courses, Bill Rogers describing the moment of losing it as 'going from guts to gob'. The red mist descends and our worst impulses become ammunition for our heaviest weapons. Stress affects cognition. Parts of the brain that have not developed since we crawled out of the sea (you know, the bits that enjoy *Jackass* and *Naked Attraction*) take over from the rational brain and we become, well, stupid. So stupid that we think howling in a teenager's face and covering him in a fine spray of coffee spittle will win him over.

Our son, Owen, who is now a terrific adult, struggled through a difficult adolescence, learning new and different ways to wind up his dad. Owen was so good at this that whenever I sought to talk to him, I very quickly became a functioning moron. I should have walked away and taken some deep breaths. This would have prevented me from venting pure nonsense that only made matters worse. I should have used a script; it would have enabled me to state fact rather than vent fury. If we use scripts often enough, there is a good chance that we can leave the reptilian brain in the primordial soup and say something more constructive.

Reframing

How you frame the situation is massive. Metaphors dictate the way we think. The lesson might look like a jungle, a threatening environment where you are constantly ambushed by hostile creatures, or you might think of it as a garden where you dig the boundaries, plant the seeds and water the plants that you want to see. How you frame the classroom situation will affect what you see and how you feel about it. If, when you stand in front of your nightmare class, you see it as a battle, where you are locked in mortal combat with Jake, Dylan and Chantelle, think again. They are kids. You are an adult. Rather than imagine yourself in the thick of hand-to-hand fighting with a deadly foe, reframe it. Think of yourself as behaviour coach. Your charges are learning to behave, just as they are learning to spell, do algebra or French. You do not get emotionally involved when they get the spelling, algebra or French wrong. So long as you have high expectations, established routines and inevitable consequences in place, you can become less emotionally affected by your pupils' behaviour.

In your first few seconds with a new class, they will subject you to the 'with-it-ness' test (see Chapter 6). They will make an assessment: is this adult on the ball? Can we get one over on them? If you begin by scanning the room, you can demonstrate that you are aware, that you know what is going on. OK, you have not worked out how to change it yet, but that will come. Right now, if someone throws an object, you will see it, and that counts.

Be aware of your emotional state

I recently visited a lesson where a trainee maths teacher was struggling to control his emotions as well as the class. Here are some of the notes I wrote for him:

▪ Make sure you remove any emotion when correcting behaviour. 'Take a seat, thank you' sounds much calmer than 'Sit down'. The former sounds like a relaxed invitation, while the latter is a desperate command.

▪ Teach them the behaviours that you want them to show you. Do not waste time complaining about it or asking why they are getting it wrong. Simply tell them what you want. Instead of, 'Why are we shouting out?' simply repeat, 'One voice, thank you.' It does not matter why they are shouting out, so do not ask.

■ At one point, when a child argued back, you said, 'I don't care, stop talking.' I sympathise, but I am a little uncomfortable hearing a teacher say, 'I don't care.' Try fogging (or, in other words, giving a non-committal response) followed by a description of the behaviour you want. For example, 'That's as maybe, I need you to listen' or 'I hear what you say, I need you to listen.' If you demonstrate that you cannot be blown off course, there will be less arguing back.

■ On another occasion you said in exasperation, 'This is ridiculous!' That is your internal monologue and it needs to stay internal. Sharing your innermost thoughts is a bad idea, as who knows what you might come out with? It is in your interest to focus on the positives since you will get more of what you notice.

■ Make sure you address the right problem. The issue today was not that Ruby and co. were chatting or chewing. It was that they weren't engaged in learning. Make this your aim rather than merely stopping the 'bad' behaviour. They did not seem bothered by the prospect of an 'amber' or a 'red'. Using these threats to dampen down their behaviour is not the same as insisting that they engage with the lesson. Your style and tone when dealing with them will help. How else might you make maths more appealing to the girls?

■ Be precise about what you want. When you say, 'Joseph, I need you to be quiet,' I think you would be better advised to say, 'Joseph, I need you to *listen*.' In that way, what may seem like a gagging order becomes an invitation to participate.

■ You need to be consciously teaching the behaviours you want to see. If you are, you will remember to state things positively – for example, rather than, 'We need to stop being rude' you will say, 'I need you to be respectful.' Thus, you will be teaching a behaviour you do want to see rather than just dampening down the behaviours you do not want to see.

■ At one point you said, 'I won't tell you again!' Why handcuff yourself? You need to be free to give as many reminders as you see fit. Statements like this are a hostage to fortune. When the child misbehaves again, you will be caught between accelerating things inappropriately and undermining yourself by failing to keep a promise.

- I would be a little more formal with them when it comes to taking turns to speak. This will preserve a calm atmosphere, and it will help to ensure that everyone contributes. Then, when Ammar shouted out, you could have said, 'One voice, thanks Ammar,' which would be less intrusive than, 'Don't comment, Ammar.' Some pupils would baulk at being 'gagged' by 'Don't comment', and a rule reminder is less provocative.

- Damian made his classmates laugh with his clowning from time to time. This was an opportunity to show that you too have a sense of humour before refocusing them – something like, 'Very good! ... You now need to ...' Instead, you called out angrily, 'Don't laugh at Damian!' which was self-defeating. As you must know, when people try to suppress laughter the outcome is usually more laughter, and your instruction sounded like, 'Don't find Damian funny!' which, I hope you will agree, is a little absurd. If you follow my advice to tell them what you do want, rather than what you do not, you can avoid falling into this trap.

Give them a reason to care

I was working with a young science teacher in the same school who was having a horrible time with Year 7. They chattered over him, ignored his instructions and generally behaved as if he was not there. When he sought to address the behaviour of individual pupils, they laughed at him. After listing all the positives I could find, I decided to level with this young man. Here is what I wrote. For the purposes of this book, it is a little more direct and less hedged about with reassurance than the original version.

Try thinking of yourself as a storyteller. Would you have kept an audience's attention today? There has to be both (a) passion – show that you are fascinated by cell walls and (b) connection – give them a reason to be fascinated by cell walls.

Today's lesson took place on Planet Science, not on the Earth where your pupils live. You need to create a bridge between the two, so that your lesson relates to the lives of these children. Here is what I came up with by thinking about cell walls:

■ What would happen to a house without walls?

■ What would happen to a human being whose cells had no walls?

Can you see how these questions help to build that bridge? You are the science teacher, and I am sure you can come up with more and probably better questions than these. ☺

Scripts

By script, I mean an organised form of words that you have thought about and practised, and that you know will be at least a measured and rational response to the behaviour with which you are faced. You need to practise these until they come out automatically.

The physical script

The first aspect of a useful script when working with children is the physical script: standing tall with a confident smile (unless you are confronted with a child having a meltdown, in which case a smile can be the worst thing you can do). If you must use a gesture, choose calm palms rather than pointy finger (if you are ever tempted to point a finger, remember there are three pointing back at you). Let empathy be your guide. How did you feel as a child when a grown-up looked at you like something on the bottom of their shoe or pointed a finger at you? Did it make you feel any more likely to comply? Think of yourself as the strong and stable adult. This means avoiding fidgeting nervously or casually draping yourself across your desk like a lounge lizard. Stand straight and ensure you are well balanced. It will help you to appear ... well, well-balanced.

Have you filmed yourself in class? Have you taken a moment to notice what your body is doing when you have the class's attention? Think about training a dog. Very few pooches will obey a command that emanates from a craven, hunched figure. Classes are the same. Stand firm, smile and establish eye contact.

Jason, a maths teacher, was talking to me once while pacing around, almost dancing about with half-suppressed anxiety. He stood up, sat down, picked up and dropped a set of books, opened and closed his desk drawer, seemingly all at the same time, and then told me, 'I just can't seem to get my classes to settle!' Small wonder, I thought. Filming yourself is a great idea, or just getting a colleague to watch you for a few minutes and give you some honest feedback can be priceless.

'The look'

Every teacher needs to have 'the look' in their armoury. You will almost certainly remember receiving this from a teacher when you were a child. On noticing that a pupil is being inappropriate, you simply turn and look. Stay perfectly still and let your eyes say 'no more'. It is not a glare, as that would signify panic and therefore weakness, and neither is it a stare; that would be weird. You are simply looking pointedly at the child for a brief moment to let them know that the behaviour must stop or you will take action.

I recently saw a teacher in Yorkshire throw 'the look' at a young person, and was horrified to see it last for several seconds while her eyes narrowed and the muscles in her face contracted. We had a good laugh about it later when I explained that her version of 'the look' was more like 'the death stare'.

Giving direction

Teachers frequently use phrases that betray their insecurity: 'Can we please listen for a moment?' You are in charge. You need the class to pay attention so that learning can take place. It might be you they need to listen to, it might be YouTube or it might be one of their peers, but whomever it is, listening is not optional and you need quiet. So, that is what you say: 'I need quiet, thank you Year 8.'

The worst behaviour policies are full of statements about what pupils 'should' do. We can all write wish lists. This language creeps into the classroom when you say, 'There should be no one talking.' Again, all these negatives complicate things, and telling them what you *don't* want fails to teach them what you *do* want, so you are better off saying, 'I need everybody listening, thank you.'

One of the verbal tics that infests the language of adults in school is the question 'OK?' Imagine some girls are chatting among themselves when they should be paying attention to your riveting description of the River Nile and its flood plain. If you say, 'Ladies, I need your attention,' that is a strong statement of fact which carries some weight. Now try, 'Ladies, I need your attention, OK?' You have effectively added, 'If that's all right with you.' It makes you sound tentative and weak. The effect is completely different.

'OK?' is a bad habit for other reasons. It is boring to hear when it is constantly repeated, and it creates the danger that by asking the class 'OK?' you might kid yourself that they understand what you have just said, simply because you said it and no one has had the bravery to raise a hand and say, 'I don't get it, miss.' 'OK?' is the enemy of effective assessment for learning.

Keep it simple

Teachers tie themselves up in verbal knots sometimes: 'Can we not touch the curtains?' All that is needed is the pupil's name and the object in question: 'Jake … the curtains … thank you.'

Sometimes a simple rule reminder will do the job: 'Jake … what am I going to say?' Notice, I do not even have to name the rule. I am just inviting Jake to remember the expectation that he is not meeting. This allows him to identify and fix the problem, and so his dignity remains intact.

When we say, 'Get the coat off, now!' we are telling the young person what the problem is, how to fix it and when. Not much room for dignity or self-respect there, so no surprise when we get a mouthful back. If Jake does not see or will not say that his coat is the problem, we can sharpen the question a little: 'Jake, what is the rule about coats?'

Say what you see

I was in a school the other day. It was blessed with those modern toilet suites where the washing basins are visible from the corridor and only the cubicle interiors are hidden from view. A boy was washing his hands. A passing behaviour manager swooped. 'Why are you in the toilets?' she barked.

The 'why' question is overused and overrated. When my son's room looked like MI6 had raided it, I sometimes got it wrong: 'Why is your room a mess?'

What was he supposed to say? Maybe 'Er … because it is?' or 'Dunno?' or any number of things, all of them likely to leave me even more annoyed and frustrated.

If Johnny has a good reason for being in the toilets, such as a medical condition, he does not deserve to be treated in this peremptory fashion. And if he does not have a good reason, barking at him is physiologically bad news, as it will wake up Johnny's reptilian brain and a hostile exchange may take place.

If only the adult had said, 'Johnny, I see you are in the toilets.' This is a statement of fact, so less likely to trigger Johnny. It would allow him either to respond easily: 'Yes miss, I've got a pass,' or to take responsibility for his behaviour: 'Sorry miss, on my way back now …' If Dwayne has his shirt hanging out, asking him 'why' is about the most pointless response I can think of. What is Dwayne mean to say? 'Because of my flagrant disregard of the rules, sir'? or 'It's my way of silently rebelling, sir, against the punitive culture that the new leadership team has created'?

If there is no good answer to the question, it is probably the wrong question.

Please and thank you

I worked for a few years at a school in Oldham which served a deprived area and could fairly be described as 'not easy'. After working with individual staff for several months, I was given the opportunity to deliver behaviour management training to the full staff.

A couple of weeks later, I was stopped on the corridor by a science teacher. 'Steve!' she said. 'That training you did. It's turned my teaching upside down!'

For a second I had an image of Bunsen burners bolted to the ceiling, and then I saw what she meant. 'In a good way I hope?'

'Yes!' she cried.

'What was it that worked for you?' I asked, hoping to be reminded of some stunningly original insight that had escaped my lips in the hall.

'I've stopped saying "please", and I've started saying "thank you"!' she cried, with evangelical fervour.

That was it. A simple change of language.

'Thank you' is so much more powerful than 'please'. It implies that you genuinely expect compliance. They say it in the military: always assume that an order will be carried out. Can you imagine a sergeant major on the parade ground shouting, 'Atteeeen-shun!' and then simpering, 'If that's all right with you?'

Saying 'thank you' rather than 'please' is a quick way to demonstrate your benign authority. 'Looking this way, please' is polite. 'Looking this way, thank you' is equally polite, but it adds so much more. You now sound as if you expect the child to do as they are told. You are not begging and you are not commanding, you are simply assuming the best.

You can repeat 'thank you' without sounding weak: 'Looking this way, thank you … (moving a little nearer) … thank you … (standing closer to the pupil, removing spectacles if you are wearing them, or perhaps raising your eyebrows and adding a little weight to the words) … *thank you*.'

Now try that again with 'please': 'Looking this way, please … (moving a little nearer) … please … (on your knees, hands clenched in supplication) … *please*!' What do you sound like?!

A secondary teacher in Bradford told me that 'thank you' did not work. Then he explained why. He had approached a pupil who had dropped a piece of litter and said, 'Thank you for picking that up.' The pupil concerned had told him where to get off.

Well, isn't that a surprise? 'Thank you' will not work if you use it like 'Open sesame' or 'Abracadabra'. It is not a magic spell that you can wield like Harry Potter's wand without any sense of context, relationship or respect. But, used carefully to show that good behaviour is not optional – it is what we genuinely expect – it really can turn your teaching upside down.

Use your own good example

A great response to unpleasant behaviour from pupils who are well known to you is to highlight your own good example – for instance, 'Have I always been respectful to you, Callum?' It is how staff in customer services at M&S do it: 'I am not raising my voice at you, sir.' I am not sure how I know this …

except there was that time I tried to return a jumper that had doubled in size in the wash. Yes, to my shame, that is probably it.

Protecting our ability to say, 'Have I always been respectful to you?' is a great reason to refrain from sarcasm with kids. If you let slip just one snarky comment, you will not be able to ask that all-important question.

Reminders

Reminders are useful so long as they are genuine. If you bark, 'Jason, *that's* your reminder!' we are back in the Harry Potter school of behaviour management, pointing at the child and shouting, 'Behaviouramus stoppus!'

It does not work. Those C1, C2, C3 systems are horrific. They have been sold to staff on the basis that 'you don't need to engage with the child, you just move them to the next C.' Brilliant: 95% of the class won't ever need to be placed on a C, and the 5% who might qualify act the way they do because the adults in their lives have not engaged with them properly, so handing out a consequence at arm's length and refusing to discuss it simply pours fuel on the flames. A reminder should be a reminder of the child's best self and a reminder of what your expectations are.

The child's best self might be: 'Last week when you worked really well and I called home to tell your mum,' or it might be: 'Your best self is really responsible, isn't it – picking up your little sister from the primary school later on? That's the "you" I need to see today.' If this is not effective you can point to the rule: 'What do we do about coats here?' and then to the consequence, if need be: 'What will happen if you keep the coat on?'

If you do apply a consequence, make it happen at all costs, but please do not rely on consequences alone to teach behaviour because they do not. As I have set out elsewhere in this book, your explicit teaching of behaviours, your modelling of them and your highlighting of them when they occur are your best ways to teach behaviour. Consequences are sometimes necessary, but be aware of their limitations.

Be precise

I often hear the phrase 'Shhh' used in classrooms, and my thought is always, as Donald Trump once said when describing a BBC correspondent, 'Here's another beauty.'[2] 'Shhh' is a problem because it says to your class, 'Do less of that' but it fails to say, 'Do *this*.' It is an all-purpose dampening down of noise that betrays your anxiety; a low-key distress signal that becomes more and more frequent until it overgrows and strangles the sense of whatever is being said. Teachers are often amazed when I tell them how many times a minute they use it. 'Shhh' is like Japanese knotweed. It must be rooted out or whatever you are trying to build will not stand.

Guiding principles when using scripts

Give it time

An essential part of any play script is the silences between the words. It was Bill Rogers who, at a course in Leeds in 1993, first introduced me to the concept of 'take-up time'. I had been appointed a head of year, so the school put me on a course. I drove to Leeds and sat in a smallish wood-panelled room with about forty others. Bill Rogers appeared and was utterly, wonderfully brilliant. The best day's training you can imagine. It was engaging, practically useful, laugh-out-loud funny and, as it turned out, life-changing. I began to share this training back at school, and so my career as a behaviour trainer was born.

I met Bill Rogers some years later when he came to a Wakefield school and I was working for the local authority. He was fiddling with his laptop all alone in the hall an hour before his session was due to begin. I slipped into the room and thanked him for kick-starting my career. He was gracious but admirably uninterested in receiving my fulsome praise. Then he looked up. 'Do one thing for me, will you?' he said. I assumed he wanted a coffee or glass of water until he went on: 'Don't send parents to prison when their kids skip school.' I nodded sagely, thinking, what the hell do I say? 'Hmm,' I managed. 'We have a very punitive culture in the UK, don't we?' 'Yes, you do!' he said pointedly and returned to his fiddling. As I left the room, it occurred to me that I had just told an Australian that Britain has a punitive culture.

---

2   See https://www.bbc.co.uk/news/av/world-us-canada-38999996.

I am not suggesting that the great man's ancestors were convicts, but the irony did not escape me.

I think I had been doing it instinctively, but listening to Bill Rogers made me consciously competent. Take-up time simply means giving your direction – perhaps, 'Back on task, thanks Brian' – and then *turning away* to allow Brian to comply without you breathing down his neck. You might even make it explicit by saying, 'Time to get back on task now, Brian. I'll be back in two minutes to see how you're getting on.'

My partner Sian and I once owned a VW camper van, and it was a little rusty. At her instigation, we stood alongside the van one Saturday morning, each armed with a pot of rust repairer and a brush. Sian was at the front end of the van, nearer the road, while I dabbed away towards the rear. We had been at this for a few minutes when I noticed she was watching me. 'What's wrong?' I asked. 'That brush,' she replied. 'It's too thick.' Now, to the women reading this book, you know what men are like. Did I reply with boundless gratitude: 'Thank you, darling, that is *such* useful feedback!' No, of course not. 'No, no, it's fine,' I mumbled. 'I can manage with *this* one.'

I knew she was right, but I did not like to admit my incompetence. Just then a friend of Sian's passed by our drive and they began chatting. I was off like a shot to the garden shed, where I found a thinner brush. I needed to wait until Sian was not looking, so I could pretend to myself that using a finer brush was my idea. I was in my late forties at the time. How pathetic is that? I tell this story to illustrate that children need to be allowed their dignity. A little take-up time will give them the space to comply without feeling like they have been oppressed.

Prevention is better than cure

I was horrified when Pope Benedict announced his resignation in February 2013, not due to any religious misgivings but because we had a holiday in Rome booked for early April. I suffered visions of pilgrim-choked piazzas and gridlocked streets, full of the faithful flocking to celebrate *Habemus papam*.

I need not have worried. All was calm by the Tuesday after Easter when our plane touched down at Fiumicino. However, the Sistine Chapel did bring me face to face with my day job. It seems that even the Vatican cannot escape the age-old problem of dealing with low-level disruption. As tourists from all over the world crowded into this tiny space on that Thursday afternoon, in a kind of reverse re-enactment of the Tower of Babel, it fell to one poor unfortunate to protect its sacred purpose. In other words, he had to stop the assorted Germans, Brits, Japanese, Americans and even the occasional Italian from talking too loudly.

Every few seconds his raking 'Shhhhh!' spread across the room, to little effect, and every couple of minutes I heard his musical cry of 'Silenzio!' I could not see him, of course; the place was too full. Anyway, the effect of 'Silenzio!' wore off pretty quickly. Hardly a surprise; you put a few hundred people in a small room under the world's most beautiful ceiling and what happens? They want to talk. What about? Well, they might be making telling points about Michelangelo's choice of colour, or they might be saying, 'Gee Hank, that must be a hundred years old!' or, as in my case, 'My bloody neck is killing me!' Whatever it is, they want to talk.

As he progressed from 'Silenzio!' to a staccato handclap, it struck me that this poor under-assistant to the deputy cardinal's gopher, or whatever he was, had a lot in common with the average supply teacher faced by a group that had no interest in him, no clear idea about exactly how much talking was too much, no thought of any consequences and thus no intention of complying with his despairing appeals. So, there is a lesson for us in leading learning when low-level disruption occurs: expectations must be clear.

The meaning of 'intrusive'

Bill Rogers came up with a great way of looking at teacher interventions, describing them as going from 'least to most intrusive'.[3] I learned my lesson about being too intrusive during a spell working with the single homeless in London's East End in the 1980s. It was a cold, dark November evening. The St George's men's care centre was a place where 'dossers', as they called themselves, could get tea or coffee, soup and a roll in the evenings for next to nothing.

One day a stranger walked in. He wore a car coat, smart trousers, a trilby hat and black eye-patch. He looked mean. I had been told he had a bottle

---

3   Bill Rogers, *You Know the Fair Rule: Strategies for Making the Hard Job of Discipline in Schools Easier*, 2nd edn (London: Pitman, 1998), p. 16.

on him, which was strictly forbidden, and so, like a fool, I put my hand in his coat pocket. This was a seriously bad idea. He roared into life: 'My pockets! My fucking pockets!', and he began to stamp on the lino, very quickly. Whether it was rage or medication or both, he seemed to lose control of his legs and they hammered out a staccato pattern on the floor, a kind of jittery, war-like tap-dancing. It was deafening. He kept up the vocals too. 'My pockets! My fucking pockets!' Of course, this man's pockets were all he had. A hand in the pocket is inappropriate at the best of times, but in this situation, well, it is hard to think of anything more intrusive.

I learned there and then that showing respect and safeguarding dignity are one and the same thing.

Always aim to de-escalate

Another thing happened one evening at St Georges men's care centre that taught me a lesson about behaviour. I was working with my colleague, Julian, buttering bread rolls and heating up the soup. It was a quiet session until a smartly dressed stranger strode in. He had beige shoes, beige trousers and a red V-neck sweater. His hair was neat. His trousers were creased. I instantly smelled danger. The men's care centre was a dark, smelly hole. No one from the civilised world would bother the place unless they were on a mission. You could say that Julian and I were, and I could tell straight away that this fellow was too, only it was not that kind of a mission. He made a beeline for Kenny.

Kenny and Gerry were a couple and they 'skippered' (slept rough) in the minister's greenhouse. Gerry, a Scot in his late sixties, wore a flat cap, kept himself to himself and did no harm to anyone. Kenny was younger, a Londoner, with a huge shock of ginger hair outlining his purple face. He was a sweet character. We had bumped into him on the street earlier in the week. 'You got a light?' he asked. My colleague Neil gave him a light. Kenny's next question: 'You got a fag?'

Anyway, this intruder, whose name turned out to be Charlie, appeared without warning, marched straight up to Kenny and thumped him. One punch sent Kenny reeling backwards until he collapsed against the far wall. It was like a scene from a Wild West saloon. Julian leapt over the counter and got right in Charlie's face, frowning and waving his finger. Bad move. I got there quick, gently moved Julian aside and adopted my best soothing voice: 'Good evening. I'm sure you can understand, we can't allow that sort of thing here. I'm sorry, but I will need to ask you to leave now, thank you.'

Of course, what I meant was, 'You've had your fun, now piss off!' but I managed to say it in a way that Charlie accepted, and off he went without any fuss. He had done what he set out to do and, to our relief, he was prepared to leave it at that. The memory of this incident came in handy during my teaching career. St George's was a good place to cut my teeth in terms of behaviour management.

Verbal abuse

While the nightmare scenario is raging, you might be subjected to verbal abuse. My advice is never, ever let this go. Verbal abuse should always be acted upon. However, your response does not have to happen now and it does not need to be punitive. In Chapter 5, I will talk in detail about Alison who called me 'Spotty'. I might have demanded a grovelling apology in front of a senior colleague, but what would that have achieved? As we will see, sitting down with her one-to-one was far more effective than any carpeting could have been.

So, when you are subjected to verbal abuse, follow it up. But do remember that you are the calm adult and they are the distressed child. We need to channel the wise old grandparent, not the hassled mum or dad. That means looking beyond the moment and seeing the journey of the young person as the most important aspect – more important than our feelings. And we must not be knocked off our perch by what an 11-year-old thinks of us. Even if a 15-year-old tells us to 'fuck off!' does it really have to ruin our day?

I have been verbally abused and I have been shoved a couple of times, and I did not enjoy it. But I did not refuse to teach the pupil concerned. They had just demonstrated very powerfully that they needed to learn, they needed a role model, they needed to feel safe and they needed to have boundaries set. I was not going to be of much use to them if I left the field of play.

As I have said, you should never ignore verbal abuse, but you do not need to demand a pound of flesh. You are bigger than that.

Finally, a sense of humour

I am reminded of the funniest moment of my teaching career. Maybe you had to be there, but it is a treasured memory. I was a Year 10 form tutor, and one of my pupils, Janet, was a real corker of a girl: brilliant, good humoured, helpful. You would be thrilled if she was your daughter, and you would be equally thrilled if your child brought her home for dinner. Janet's name came after her friend Helen's in the register, and one day I accidentally left out Helen's name and went straight to Janet's. Without missing a beat, Janet looked up and said, with mock indignation, 'Oh? Fuck Helen, then!'

Thirty years later, I can still see the shock in Janet's eyes as she realised what had just escaped her mouth, and her hand clamped over it, too late. The form collectively held its breath. I raised an eyebrow. 'Janet?' I deadpanned. 'I need a word at the end of this registration.' My faint smile let the class know that I too found it hilarious, but I was not going to let Janet off the hook entirely – not just yet. The room burst into laughter which quickly subsided and the register continued.

As the class dispersed, Janet arrived at my desk, the colour of beetroot. I looked up at her and smiled. 'Janet? Did you forget where you were just now?' She was too embarrassed to speak but nodded hastily, mouthed a 'thank you' and made her way to lesson one. I have been hard on myself in this book, but I am going to blow my own trumpet here. I had the confidence not to panic at the sound of a taboo word, and the common sense to see that poor Janet had simply forgotten herself. Her mortification was proof that she intended no disrespect to me or anyone else. The classmates knew that some of my colleagues would have thrown their rattle out of the pram in this circumstance, and I went up in their estimation simply because I did not.

Responding effectively to poor behaviour when it happens is a vital group of skills to possess. However, it is in a sense a sticking plaster; the poor behaviour you are faced with may emanate from longer term elements that you can influence, if not control. What really matters is that these factors – such as your relationship with the pupil and the class, your modelling of the behaviours you want to see and your classroom routines – are as they should be. The rest of this book deals with these factors which will bring you long-term success more reliably.

Takeaways

- We cannot control children; they do not come with a remote control. Leading behaviour is a more subtle and long-term process.

- Always look to be as least intrusive as possible, and always aim to de-escalate.

- Give yourself thinking time. Take a moment to contemplate the bigger picture.

- State facts about established expectations and routines. Avoid displays of emotion as this will incentivise further misbehaviour.

- Do not take yourself too seriously. Protect the well-being and dignity of your pupils with as much vigour as you guard your own.

NOW TRY THIS:

Turn to Appendix 4. Choose three of the responses listed there and apply them in your lesson tomorrow. Watch closely. How do your pupils respond?

Chapter 3

STYLES

In Chapter 1, I challenged you to think about what you believe, about the values you hold dear and how these will be your anchor in the behaviour storm. I now want you to look at your own behaviour by comparing various styles and approaches. To what extent do you care or control? Do you behave more like a parent, an adult or a child? Do you tend to be proactive or reactive when it comes to leading behaviour? By examining your own actions, you will be able to see where it both enables and frustrates your desire to lead pupil behaviour effectively in the classroom.

Care and structure

Some years ago, I sat back and wondered, after watching all these teachers do the job, what was it that seemed to work? On the one hand, it seemed to have something to do with how much structure they provided, and on the other, how much they appeared to care about young people. That led me to the figure that I have reproduced on the following page.

In his book *Restorative Practice*, Mark Finnis has created something very similar.[1] His axes are 'support' and 'challenge', which is a great way for schools to analyse the approach that the whole school takes towards its pupils. Although my diagram is different, it will certainly seem familiar to readers of his book and those who have attended Mark's inspirational training. I am using it with his blessing, I am pleased to say.

---

1   Finnis, *Restorative Practice*, p. 53.

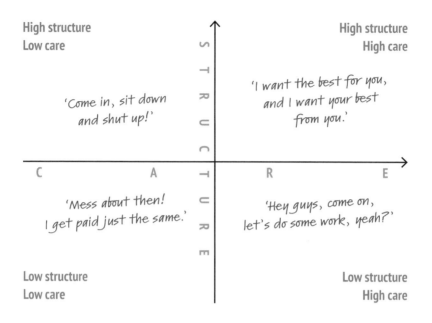

High structure
Low care

High structure
High care

S
T
R
U
C

'Come in, sit down
and shut up!'

'I want the best for you,
and I want your best
from you.'

C   A   R   E

T
U
R
E

'Mess about then!
I get paid just the same.'

'Hey guys, come on,
let's do some work, yeah?'

Low structure
Low care

Low structure
High care

The structure–care grid

High structure/low care

I witnessed the high structure/low care approach most recently when visiting an RE lesson in South Yorkshire. I entered the room along with the last few stragglers and found an empty seat at the back. The lights were off and the blinds were down. A sinister glow from the whiteboard was all that kept us from total darkness. No one moved. The teacher was petite; in fact, I only picked her out amid the gloom when she began to speak. Her voice, though, was thunderous: 'You will SIT down! You will NOT talk! You have DONE the revision, you have GOT your books and there is NO reason to speak to ANYONE! If you DO so much as WHISPER, I will SEND for on-call, and YOU will be in BIG TROUBLE! (She paused to reload) IS THAT CLEAR?!'

I don't know how the class felt, but I was scared witless! It reminded me of Mr Bown's science lab in the 1970s. Mr Bown – or Pinhead as we called him, due to his tiny bonce that swivelled like a searchlight atop a sky-scraping body – was so terrifying that one of my classmates fainted in his lesson

and another one peed himself. Every lesson was seventy minutes of pri-
mal fear, subsiding for a few minutes only halfway through when Pinhead
retreated to his prep room to smoke a cigarette and watch us via a mirror.
(Yes, really.) Mr Bown's general science lessons were recorded as 'GenSci' in
my timetable, but looking at it, I could not have experienced greater fear
and revulsion if my timetable read 'GenTorture' or 'GenPain'.

Back at RE, with this woman's take-no-prisoners approach, I had to remind
myself that I was in twenty-first-century Sheffield, not twentieth-century
Ilford. Any notion that a religious education lesson might possibly be linked
to enlightenment, spirituality or, dare I say it, love, had clearly bypassed this
teacher altogether. Thanks to Mr Bown, I dropped all the sciences at the
end of Year 9, which you could do then. Now, I am fascinated by science;
I could listen to Professor Brian Cox talk about the cosmos for hours, but
as a child I learned to associate science with fear, just as – thanks to my
PE teachers – I came to associate physical education with humiliation and
pain. I wonder how many of that class will go on to study RE at GCSE?

Some cynical staff will tell you that this uber-strict approach works. Perhaps we should debate what 'works' means? Fear might temporarily bolt
the pupils to their desks and wire their jaws shut. However, frightened
children do not learn very well. It will not instil a lifelong love of learning either. Fear, resentment and the desire for revenge is a powerful brew
which becomes a toxic mix when left to curdle in a classroom. What goes
around will inevitably come around. Plus, once you have fired your tactical
nuke in response to a bit of chatter, where do you go when something really
bad happens? Shouting at children teaches them that the way to deal with
problems is verbal violence, and that is a very big boomerang to launch
out into your classroom. We must be the stable, resilient adults at all costs.

If I am not winning you over right now, if you deal in draconian discipline
dished out at arm's length, I must refer you to a senior member of the West
Yorkshire fire service, who spoke to me after I gave my behaviour management presentation to his assembled officers in 2007, hoping to inform their
work with disaffected youth. This tall, craggy man – a cross between Sean
Bean and Clint Eastwood – approached, looked down at me and, I will be
honest, I was a little worried about what he was going to say. But I need
not have: 'You know, son, you're dead right. We used to do discipline the old
way. And what did that leave us with? A bunch of immaculately disciplined
fire fighters who couldn't think for themselves.'

In the early years of this century, Chinese civil servants visited Britain wanting to know how we did behaviour in schools. The reason was simple: children in China were extremely obedient, but they were also severely lacking in key employability skills. A different approach was needed to foster the creative skills needed in a dynamic economy. It might be convenient for us if our pupils sit mute, chained to desks for twenty-five hours a week, but it will not serve the needs of society.

My fellow grammar school boys and I were groomed to become the civil servants who would sit pushing pens for forty years, in subservience to those from private schools who would be governing the country. There is not much call for pen-pushers these days or people to process a cheque, for example. As Dylan Wiliam has pointed out, the routine cognitive jobs are going the same way that so many unskilled manual jobs went.[2] The future of employment lies in jobs that a computer cannot do, so interpersonal skills will be where it's at. A classroom where there are accepted established routines and expectations, where everyone has a say and all are respected is going to produce more useful citizens than the laboratories of fear that I endured in my youth.

Low structure/high care

At the opposite end of the spectrum, low structure/high care, are those teachers who start out wanting to be the kids' friend. Peter was teaching French in Leeds. Thirty Year 8 pupils were interrupting his every sentence, messing about and generally acting as if he was not there. 'Guys, guys!' he pleaded constantly. When he took the register, he must have paused it a dozen times, answering every question that was thrown at him. Then he got up and buzzed about the room like a big friendly bear exuding positivity, but no one was learning anything because he simply had not got a grip on them. The chatter and off-task behaviour rolled on. This approach could not last, and it did not. After half an hour, Peter suddenly yelled, 'Right, I have HAD enough! You are NOT working. You are MESSING ABOUT. There is TOO MUCH TALKING and I am FED UP with it.' Sound familiar? We are back in the low care/high control category. Without routine, structure, boundaries

---

2   Dylan Wiliam, *Embedded Formative Assessment* (Bloomington, IN: Solution Tree Press, 2011).

and consequences, Peter's high level of care could not be sustained, and his approach flipped.

I worked with Peter for a series of lessons and found myself puzzled by his apparent inability to assert himself in the classroom – until it hit me. It was not that he could not be assertive, it was that *he did not want to*. In conversation that day, Peter opened up to me about childhood experiences that had led him to equate being in command with being cruel. Guided by this revelation, we were able to make progress. Peter found ways to be in charge that did not trigger his own bad feelings, and his classroom management was transformed.

Peter is not the only one. Your experience of school can affect the way you see things. My own school days had been something of a nightmare. I spoke 'nicely', the way my mother had drilled into me, and I would do anything to avoid crossing the teachers because I was so scared of my mother's reaction. I used to correct the other boys' grammar: 'It's not I *ain't*, it's I *have not*!' Admit it, you would have thumped me, wouldn't you? I was bullied from the moment I stepped inside a school at the age of 5 until I was 13. So, when I returned to school twenty years later as a teacher, receiving the approbation of school pupils felt incredibly good, like slipping into a warm bath. I was back in school, and this time I was popular! My euphoria did not last long. For every Year 7 pupil who fell for my wit and wisdom, there was a hardened 15-year-old who regarded me, initially, as another useless adult come to fail them, in every sense. It took me a while to work out that children did not need an extra friend; what they needed was a warm, empathetic adult they could trust. I got there in the end, but not without much heartache and some incident. In teaching, you have to learn, fast.

Low structure/low care

The worst of all possible worlds is low structure/low care. 'Mess about then – I get paid just the same!' is the most cowardly way out. It is also quite naive. If the head teacher finds out, you might not be paid for much longer. I saw a supply teacher in Bradford who was so hateful to the children, so aggressive and full of bitter complaints – until he gave up and sulked in a corner – that I sought out the head teacher and begged him to remove this man from the company of children as soon as possible. I am a behaviour coach, not an Ofsted inspector, but it was as plain as day: this character was toxic to be around. I pride myself on helping established as well as new teachers to turn it around, but with this guy? I could work with him until judgement day, and he would still be in the wrong job.

A very different example of the low structure/low care approach was a supply teacher who used to visit the Sheffield school where I taught. She was in her late forties, very well spoken and often well dressed in a pleated skirt and expensive blue jumper, with a pearl necklace and earrings to match – very much a Tory lady from the Shires. She used to carry her register in a wicker basket; in fact, she looked more prepared for alfresco dining with André Rieu and his orchestra than Year 9 English.

Smoked salmon and Prosecco may not have been in the basket, but the *Telegraph* was. She would sit at the teacher's desk, unfold her newspaper, which was broad enough to occupy her entire field of vision, and let chaos reign for the duration. With the *Telegraph* for protection she was quite serene, or at least she was until another colleague had reason to intrude. How many times have I walked into a classroom only to see the teacher leap out of their chair? There are times, of course, when letting the class be is the right thing to do. But if you find yourself wanting to sit and chill when you know you should really be out among your pupils helping them learn, it is time to ask yourself some hard questions. Is your content stale? Is your approach predictable? Do you still like kids?

High structure/high care

And so we enter the Promised Land. The teacher cares, and backs up that care with structures that keep pupils safe and engaged. There are routines and boundaries in place. Good effort, achievement and behaviour are recognised. Poor behaviour attracts other inevitable consequences. The teacher, just like Peter, wants to do his best for the pupils, but he also demands the best from each pupil. You might sum this up for a child like this:

I want the best for you. You know I do because of:

- My refusal to bear grudges. Every day is a new day and a new start for all my pupils.

- My *joie de vivre.* Watching me teach, it is obvious that I love the job and I love children.

- My thorough planning of engaging, relevant content.

- My listening ear that is always available outside of lesson time, if you have a problem you need to share.

For all these reasons, and more, you know I want the best for you. And I want your best from you too.

Parent, child or adult?

If you have read *I'm OK – You're OK*, the seminal 1960s handbook of trans-actional analysis written by Thomas Harris[3] (no, not the one who wrote *The Silence of the Lambs* – that would be *I'm OK – You'd Taste Better with a Fine Chianti*), you will find a way of looking at relationships that underpins how we act in the classroom. I thoroughly recommend reading the book but, to summarise, it proposes that there are three parts to your personality: parent, child and adult. It is instructive to reflect on them and consider which of the three is dominant in your classroom persona.

Parent

The parent can be nurturing and supportive, of course, but it tends to want its own way too. The parent tells people what to do. This part of you is expressed at home when you say, 'Shut that door,' 'Put the kettle on,' 'Take off those outdoor shoes' and, typically, in the classroom, 'Sit down and open your book.' There is a place for giving direct commands, but we can tire of them. As we all know, teachers are famous for a number of things – wearing leather patches, being useful in a pub quiz and behaving like naughty children when the education secretary addresses their union conference – but their most infamous character trait is perhaps the most obvious: being bossy.

---

3   Thomas Harris, *I'm OK – You're OK: A Practical Guide to Transactional Analysis* (London: Arrow Press, 2012 [1967]).

Teachers, I am sorry to say, are notorious for being unduly controlling in social situations. Going on a hike with a teacher who insists he knows the way is bad enough. Attempting the same activity in the company of two teachers who both insist they know the way and disagree about it? I would fake illness to avoid that scenario; in fact, I think I would break my own leg to get out of it.

The parent style of teaching can be especially problematic for pupils who are suffering from adverse childhood experiences, as the trauma and neglect they have experienced marks you out as a hostile presence in their lives. One unduly sharp command is all it takes to cause an emotional melt-down, which is why certain scripts can be lifesavers. For example, instead of, 'Sit down!' try saying, 'Sitting down, thank you.' It removes the verbal pointed finger that you were metaphorically thrusting into the child's rib cage. You will need to practise, perhaps with pupils who are a tad less combustible, until you feel natural saying it.

I watched a young maths teacher recently struggling to placate two girls in his Year 8 class who would blow up at the slightest provocation. Among all the other advice I gave him, I told him to think about acting less like a demanding parent and a little more like a wise old grandparent. Try distraction and surprise them with kindness; an arm around the shoulder is so much more productive than a metaphorical (or real) finger in the face. To succeed in teaching, you do need a little of the devil in you, by which I mean that you must be prepared to impose your will on the room, and there are many ways to do it without being a half-crazed authoritarian, which we will examine as we go along.

Child

The child can be playful and creative, but in this context the child is the part of your personality that expresses its needs. We hear it in our children on car journeys when they squeal, 'Are we nearly there yet?' and we hear it in ourselves when we say, 'I've had just about enough of this!' or 'How many times do I have to tell you?' If a pupil replies to that question with, 'Um, I think it might be five or possibly six?' what would you say to them? Autistic children and those on the spectrum may not understand your rhetorical questions. And what do you look and sound like when you complain about your unmet needs? Not that great, I will wager.

We all have an internal monologue, and it is best kept internal, yet I frequently hear staff tell their classes, 'Well, this lesson started all right, but it's all gone downhill in the last ten minutes!' If you have you ever told a class, 'I'm getting very annoyed now!' bear in mind that this roughly translates as, 'That thing you're doing to wind me up; it's working!' Would Roger Federer shout across the net, 'I'm finding it really hard to return your serves to my forehand'? Of course not. A class is a pack animal; you do not want to signal weakness to it.

There is no possible advantage to be gained by behaving in this way. We need to keep a positive dialogue going, which is why noticing and praising those getting it right is so valuable and so much better than focusing our attention on what is going wrong.

Adult

The adult is the part of your personality that states fact. The best way to describe it is in comparison to the other two. Thinking back to when my daughter was 10 years old and had recently become one of those vegetarians who will not eat vegetables:

- In parent mode, I would have given an instruction: 'Get that eaten!'

- In child mode, I would have expressed my needs: 'I'm so sick of having this conversation, why can't you just eat the broccoli?'

- In adult mode, I would state fact: 'When you've eaten the broccoli, then you can have your ice cream.'

It does not take a genius to see which was most effective. The theory of transactional analysis is that life is a see-saw. Imagine that at the top of the see-saw's arc is 'parent' and at the bottom 'child'. When the see-saw is parallel to the ground it is at 'adult'. So if you act *up* in parent mode, you push the other person *down* into child mode. In the classroom, this sounds like this:

Teacher (*up in parent mode*): Put that away!

Pupil (*pushed down into child mode*): It weren't me!

If, on the other hand, you act in child mode in the classroom it can look like this:

> Teacher (*down in child mode*): Oh, I wish you'd behave! How many times do I have to ...?
>
> Child (*pushed up into parent mode, telling you what to do*): Fuck off!

If you can stay in adult mode, stating a fact such as, 'Jason, there's a school rule about equipment,' you might get a better response as you are not setting off the see-saw into a parent–child tizzy.

Readers who are in a relationship might be able to think about a row you have had and track back to see how going to one extreme or the other may have triggered a response you did not want.

What behaviours wind me up?

Several years ago, I was teaching on supply at a Leeds secondary school. On arrival, I was told that I had no lesson in period four. I should report to reception at that time and they would 'find me something'. This sounded ominous, and indeed proved to be so. At 11.15am, I was collected by the behaviour manager, who led me to the referral room where I found two sullen children and a young head of department. 'You can get off if you like, Glyn,' said my tall companion. 'This gentleman will be staying here this hour.' Glyn was delighted; in fact, he seemed so overwhelmed by his good fortune I thought he was going to cry. He grabbed his books, pen, sandwiches, diary and practically skipped and danced out of the room. Both inmates registered his leaving with barely a flicker of interest and remained studiedly motionless, like two lazy lions on a hot day in London Zoo.

'These people are here all day,' said the behaviour manager. 'Bethany has to go for her jab at 11.05am, and at 11.50am they have a toilet visit. If either of them wants to go, you've all got to go, and just wait in the corridor. Any problems, ring reception – the number is on the wall behind you.'

The girl, Year 9 at a guess, sat nearest. She toyed with her peroxide hairdo and showed intermittent interest in a worksheet that had been placed under her nose, until she was collected for her jab, leaving me alone with the boy. He decided to ignore the work and fix me with a stare. I raised my eyebrows in acknowledgement. Then he began clicking his pen. Click, click, click-ick, click. Determined to ignore this transparent ploy to wind me up, I opened the Scrabble app on my phone and started a new game, until my contemplation of what to do with A-A-I-I-O-R-U was disturbed once more. Click-ick ick, click-ick, click. Then a pause. Then a resumption. The one thing I must not do is rise to this, I told myself. It is a silly schoolboy trick to rile an adult with something so innocuous. I must not rise to this. I will not rise to this. I exchanged four vowels and got another three in my replacement letters. Click, click, ick, click.

Like Oscar Wilde, I can resist anything except temptation. 'You need to be doing your work,' I heard myself say, 'and knock it off with the pen, thanks!'

Damn. I had gone and done it. I had given this malcontent exactly what he craved.

There was a sudden hail of clicks. Click, ick, ick, ick. Click. Click. Click, ick, ick-ick ick ick. Twice as fast as before and utterly relentless. I was amazed his pen did not explode. Of course, he was going to win this confrontation that I had stupidly invited. What was I going to do? Ring reception in tears, screaming, 'He won't stop clicking his pen'? I cannot envisage Chuck Norris and a SWAT team smashing feet first through the windows to rescue me from a boy who cannot decide whether his ballpoint should be in the on or off position.

How to rescue the situation? I felt a need to be seen to allow the clicking. 'OK,' I said in tones that were as kindly, measured and sarcasm-free as I could muster. 'Click away if you like. Feel free.'

Not an episode to be proud of, but a timely reminder of how easy it is to fall prey to the traps that unhappy young people can set for us.

What behaviours wind you up? Think about some of these common occurrences:

- Talking out of turn/interrupting.
- Lack of correct equipment.
- Getting out of seat.
- Playing with objects.
- Making noises.

- Defacing work.

- Inappropriate laughter.

- Ignoring a reasonable request.

- Refusing to undertake a task.

- Answering back.

- Swearing.

- Knocking furniture about.

- Violence.

The items at the bottom this list are the low-frequency, high-intensity behaviours, which happen comparatively rarely, but we remember them because the experience is so powerful.

When the worst happens, and there is a fight in your classroom or you have been verbally abused or even physically assaulted, most schools are pretty good now about getting you some TLC and some space. This mitigates the long-term damage that such nasty events might otherwise cause. But when it is just twenty-six Year 7s who will not stop muttering while you address the class or a group of Year 10s who wander off task every two minutes, teaching can feel a very lonely occupation indeed. It is the dripping taps that do you in, not the flying chairs.

Of course, another key issue is that there may well be behaviours that are against the rules but that do not wind you up. It may not spoil your day if Damian's shirt is not tucked in, that he is quietly chewing or that he is listening to music on headphones, for example. The temptation to just ignore these things is ever-present. There are many reasons for resisting though:

- It makes life so much easier for the next member of staff who is professional enough to apply the whole school rules if she is not the first adult that day to remind Damian to tuck his shirt in.

- It is confusing for young people if adults shirk their responsibilities. What we might see as reasonable, they may see as weakness. Although they often test them, pupils appreciate boundaries.

- Teaching is a team sport and we are, as they say, *in loco parentis*. Every parent knows the importance of presenting a united front and sticking to it. You are possibly driven half-mad, as I sometimes am, by young people who keep asking long after they have been told 'no'. It goes something like this:

You: Shelly? In your usual seat, thank you.

Shelly: Oh miss! Let us stay here. We'll be good!

You: Shelly – there's your usual seat. Thank you.

Shelly: But, miss, I don't want to sit there. I want to sit with Kylie. Oh, go on, miss, let us!

You: Shelly, you know my seating plan, thank you!

Shelly: Yes, but miss …

The reason Shelly persists in this fruitless attempt to change your mind has one obvious cause: it works at home and possibly with some staff.

So, what I am saying is, whether the behaviour winds you up or not, apply the whole school expectation. This will make life easier for you and everybody else in the long run. Children love to play mum off against dad, often with stressful results for both parents. It is no surprise that they try this with their dozen or so classroom teachers, and it is imperative that you and your colleagues hold the line.

Proactive or reactive?

You know the game whack-a-mole? There is a machine at every seaside amusement park where you put in your 50p coin, the moles pop up at random and you hit them as fast as you can with a mallet. Watching Key Stage 3 classes being taught badly, I see whack-a-mole all the time – the ultimate *reactive* approach. 'Jason!' Whack. 'Dylan!' Whack. 'Kerrie-Jo!' Whack. And so on. There is no mallet being wielded, of course, but the teacher is making energetic attempts to stuff each little mole back into its hole, and failing miserably. Thirty moles and one teacher – no contest.

Classroom whack-a-mole is the inevitable product of an approach that goes like this: 'I was in the classroom with my Year 8s the other day, teaching

Romeo and Juliet, when damn me, some *behaviour* happened!' Well, there is a surprise. Too many staff do not talk about behaviour at all until it goes pear-shaped, and then they try to 'manage it'. You would not teach geography by having pupils guess the capital cities of Europe and shouting at each wrong answer, but plenty of staff teach behaviour like that – or try to. 'Behaviour' for these teachers is some kind of extraneous force or entity that sneaks into the room like a silent fart or the malicious spirit in *Paranormal Activity* and starts messing with pupils' heads, and until this (bad) behaviour manifests itself in answering back, calling out or flicking bits of rubber about, there is no need whatsoever to mention it.

This approach also entails a 'behaviour support team', who heroically remove the demon-possessed to talk them down, and a 'head of behaviour', usually an overworked assistant vice principal, who is a kind of Witchfinder General, psychotherapist, hostage negotiator, chief of police, firefighter and father/mother confessor rolled into one.

On the other hand, a *proactive* approach would mean:

- Recognising that behaviour can be a good thing that contributes to learning. Indeed, learning cannot take place without certain positive behaviours. They need to be named and taught, acknowledged and rewarded.

- Taking responsibility for the behaviour – recognising that the unseen forces at work in the room might be boredom or poor literacy or other factors over which the teacher does have some influence.

- Including behaviour for learning in the lesson objective and revisiting it in plenaries. Name the exact behaviours you want to see and then acknowledge them whenever you see them.

Finding your own style is done over months and years, not days. You will make mistakes and that is OK, so long as you learn the lessons they bring. Teachers' personal styles differ, and pupils benefit massively from the variety of adult personalities they encounter in school. Most importantly, whatever style you adopt, it must embody the right values and beliefs, and it must enable you to hold the line when it comes to chewing, headphones and other misdemeanours.

I emphasise in these pages, as others have done elsewhere, the importance of displaying empathy for the 5% whose lives have been blighted by trauma of various kinds. However, your teaching style should also be informed by empathy for the 95% – the ordinary children who will quite naturally test our boundaries from time to time. We should never be surprised by inappropriate behaviour. You might be the charismatic sort or you might possess the still, small voice that captures pupils' interest in a completely different way; whatever your style is, it must enable you to teach the behaviour you want to see, model it in your own behaviour and highlight it when you see it.

Takeaways

- Being proactive and teaching the behaviour you want to see is much more effective than being reactive.

- Stating fact gets better results than ordering children around or complaining to them.

- Be aware of the behaviours that wind you up. Know what your 'buttons' are and make sure they are out of sight.

NOW TRY THIS:

Plot yourself on the structure–care grid on page 44. Ask a trusted colleague to do the same for you. Do your answers match? What action points occur to you?

Think of three statements that you tend to make in class that are parental or childlike. Write an adult script to replace them. Try using this script in class and see what difference you make.

Chapter 4

ROUTINES

I meet teachers with levels of personal organisation that range from totally sorted to calamitously unsorted. Pupils make a snap judgement when a new adult enters the room. Is this guy on top of things, or not? They can sniff out uncertainty at thirty paces, so having your stall set out is crucial. I am constantly amazed by the number of behaviour leaders in schools who are or have been PE teachers. I put this down to two things. Firstly, the process of getting fit necessarily involves focusing not on what you are but on what you might be (yes, we are back at the growth mindset). Secondly, and perhaps more importantly, a PE teacher who does not have their bibs and cones organised is stuffed. PE teachers get their ducks in a row or they get other careers. It is that simple.

The best classroom routines flow from our values, which gives them purpose. For example, I chose to implement a random seating plan on the first day with a new class because I wanted my pupils to know that I was in charge and that they were all equal in my eyes. The first thing I did was to distribute books, taking care to model a respectful approach to them. I gave out the books and other resources with a courteous, attentive manner. I wanted the children to know that respect was the first routine, and I knew that showing them respect would be much more effective than telling them about it. This was how we would routinely treat each other in future. Once we got to know each other, of course, there would be plenty of banter and a lot of good-spirited mickey-taking, but we always had that bedrock of respect to fall back on.

Organised – to be or to do?

It took me a long time to realise that organisation is more than just a trait that you either do or do not have. It is something you *do*. I suffered for years because I thought 'organised' was an adjective, unaware that with the removal of just one letter it becomes a verb – organise!

I believed that I was disorganised, just like I was left-handed and 5 feet, 8 inches tall. (Well, 5 foot, 7 and ¾ inches, but you get my point.) Misled by my infant schoolteachers, who named me 'The Absent-Minded Professor', I saw chaos and confusion as an immutable fact about me, not a habit I could change. In fact, organised people do things that make them that way; they invest time in creating systems that work for them and routines that maintain their systems.

I was slow to grasp this fact, but eventually realisation dawned; my days would be forever blighted by balls-ups and angry line managers unless I changed. So, I did the spadework. I put in the time and slowly taught my butterfly brain to travel in straight lines, planning, checking, double-checking and even (whisper it) finishing one thing before starting the next.

Sadly, I am still prone to the odd lapse, such as boarding the wrong train at King's Cross a few years ago. We pulled out of the station five minutes earlier than I had expected, and as the dreadful truth sank in, I had the dubious pleasure of asking the woman opposite me, 'Excuse me. I'm sorry to bother you, but would you mind telling me where we're going?'

That might be a metaphor for my entire career, but that is for another book.

Taking the register

Taking the register is a good example of a situation you will meet that requires a robust routine. After all, it is the single most important part of your lesson. That may sound surprising, but parents' most basic requirement of us is that we know where their kids are and that we keep them safe. For decades, teachers tended to forget that until the bar was raised with the safeguarding agenda and the work that was done to improve attendance in the early 2000s. Now, all good leadership teams ensure the register is taken in every lesson. Watching a teacher register their pupils tells me a great deal about them, about how organised they are and how effectively they teach the behaviour they want to see.

Questions to address include:

- **When will you take the register?** As soon as you have welcomed the class, or just before the ten-minute deadline that SLT have warned you about? Unless you have decided this, you risk forgetting to send it. Do you want the attendance officer bursting into your classroom, frazzled and furious, reminding you, through gritted teeth, of your responsibilities, while your class lose the plot?

- **How will you do it?** Will you use a bright, optimistic tone or will you sound as if you are listing your allergies? Will you say 'Good morning' or 'Good afternoon' to every child? Are you one of those Spanish teachers who insists on getting a 'Hola' out of every last child, even if it is the only word of target language they say that day?

- **How should pupils respond?** Will you insist on a pleasant bright 'Yes miss/sir' or will a surly 'Here' suffice? I have always insisted on the former, not because I am on a power trip but because it sets the right tone. It is a verbal sign that we are all sitting up and taking notice.

- **What will your class be doing?** Will they be sitting in silence, or should they be getting on with an engager activity while you call the names?

The register is a legal document and it is how we keep children safe. But it is also a ritual, marking the transition from social to learning time; it is a moment when, by definition, every pupil is noticed; and it is a note of formality, providing a benign reminder to all those present of the relationship of authority that exists between teacher and pupils. Getting the register right will set you on the path to success. It is that important.

Being organised: Mrs Thatcher and the Good Samaritan

I do not often quote Margaret Thatcher, Britain's first female prime minister, not a woman known for her easy charm or boundless empathy, but when I think about being organised, Mrs T's unique interpretation of the parable of the Good Samaritan comes to mind. He was able to help, she said, because he had the cash.[1] I always found this a rather bizarre way to look at the story but, undeniably, he was in a position to help.

Imagine it is Tuesday morning break, your duty morning, a fact that slipped your mind last week when you promised Year 9 a practical science lesson after break. Your duty is at the far end of the school, so by the time you make it back, the class have been lining up for five minutes and behaviour is getting ragged. On reaching the lab, you remember that their books are in the staff workroom. You send Parveen off to get them while you referee a dispute between Nita and Bobbie-Anne about a pen-top. Now you realise that you have forgotten to book the visualiser, which your head of department is using with her Year 11 group. Harvey, Lisa and Wayne are arguing over who has to sit next to Brandon. After much faffing about, the books have arrived and you are ready to begin, so you gather them around for your demonstration. Now, where did you put those safety specs?

Are you in a position to help?

Routines that teach behaviour

Do you find yourself expending energy in a fruitless struggle to persuade children to behave? Using established routines is far more effective. If you plan, rehearse and apply routines for all the behaviours you want, you will have a much easier time of it than if you rely on force of personality – or, God help you, try to reason with a pack of 13-year-olds.

The same applies to younger children. For example, I saw a Year 3 teacher recently, in Wolverhampton, who wanted the class to listen to a pupil's

---

1   See https://www.margaretthatcher.org/document/104210.

answer: 'Come on everybody, let's listen to what Angie has to say. Please … can we be respectful? … Everyone? … Please?' It was painful to watch her struggle. Trying to persuade children of the moral case for shutting up is almost impossible as well as unnecessary. She might simply have said, and repeated, 'One voice, thank you' – a simple reminder of an accepted way that we do things here. There is no pleading or threatening involved; in fact, no emotion whatsoever, simply a statement of fact. That is a lot less taxing on the batteries, and if, commendably, you want to link the routine to values, something like, 'Respect one voice, thank you' will do, but this is a routine reminder, not moral persuasion. The point is to make behaviour automatic.

Another teacher in the same school told his class that 'I shouldn't hear any talking.' This naming of unwanted behaviours is counter-productive. I do not suppose he wanted to see any belly-dancing or knife-throwing either, so why did he not outlaw these behaviours? When politicians receive media training they are told, 'Do not talk about a pink elephant,' meaning that, if the Opposition are obsessed with the threat of inflation, do not use the word 'inflation' yourself because putting it in the mind of your audience is doing the Opposition's work for them. In 2022, Penny Mordaunt did exactly this, repeating her opponent's description of the prime minister in a manner that both defended her boss and shoved the knife in at the same time.[2]

By the same token, if you say to someone in the third row, 'Stop playing with that,' you are talking about a pink elephant. Why tell the class that some pupils are playing with things? Others will now crane to look. 'What was Eric playing with?' the class wag might speculate aloud, and then the class will break up laughing and your lesson will sink with all hands. If instead you had simply used the pupil's name and paused briefly, giving them 'the look' (as described in Chapter 2), this would have excited less curiosity; for now, suffice to say that every teacher needs one. The key point to remember is this: we should avoid describing unwanted behaviour at all costs since, to use a phrase that Paul Dix taught me, 'You get more of what you notice.'

Instead of saying, 'I shouldn't hear any talking,' that teacher in Wolverhampton might simply say, 'Quiet working, thanks.' He would be describing the behaviour he wants to see, making it far more likely to happen. 'Quiet working, thanks' would be a reminder to the class of an established routine for quiet working. This routine would, of course, need an investment of time to

2   See https://www.youtube.com/watch?v=Tq14nG5-mvc.

establish it, but, forever after, a light-touch reminder of this positive expectation would do the job.

The first five minutes

Developing this thought about pupils following suit, let us look at the start of the lesson. When I am coaching a teacher, I like to be there when the lesson begins. First impressions, as the song goes, are lasting impressions. The question in my mind is, how effectively does the first five minutes of this teacher's lesson teach their class the behaviour they want to see?

Meet and greet

The 'meet and greet' is a vital part of your routine. If at all possible, arrive before your pupils do. Yes, there will be days when stuff happens, and also the timetable might necessitate you walking half a mile from one block to another during one or two lesson changeovers a week, but for most staff, most of the time, it is usually possible to get there first. During the COVID-19 pandemic, one of the biggest issues secondary schools faced was that, in order to limit the transmission of infection, pupils stayed put and teachers moved from class to class. Pretty soon, pupils began to take ownership of these spaces. They did not exactly dig trenches but classrooms became their territory, into which staff stepped with trepidation. Anyone who has worked in schools knows that it has to be the other way around. Your classroom is your gaff, your rules.

A meet and greet is a powerful and utterly benign way to establish this. Stand in the doorway looking as if you are pleased to see your class and excited about the lesson. This demonstrates your high expectations. Have a brief, positive word for everyone. You might feel like frowning at Declan and warning him that he had better be a darn sight better than he was the other day, but there is nothing to be gained from this. Instead, a smile and a friendly word lets him know that there are no grudges here, that today, like every day, is a fresh start.

And, of course, you are pleased to see every last one of them, right? Even Dylan who has made your life a misery from day one, who treats your lesson as an opportunity to doodle, to heckle you, to tease, distract and annoy his classmates, leaving you an exhausted and self-loathing wreck three times a week. But then, one Monday morning, you overhear three wonderful words in the staffroom at morning break: 'Dylan's not in.' This heavenly prospect hits you with the force of a lottery win. You leap onto a low coffee table, punch the air and yell, 'Yesss! Thank you, God – I can *teach* today!' You dash around the room, grabbing your startled colleagues by the elbow and catching their eyes, all the time manically repeating, 'He's not in! He's not in! Oh, hallelujah!'

But Dylan's absence was only a trip to the dentist – a five-minute walk from the school – and so, that afternoon, when school restarts after lunch and you float into your classroom on your little cloud of Dylan-free joy, your balloon is burst by the sight of a certain young man walking through your door. 'Er ... Dylan? ... Hi!' you manage to say, with a politician's toothy smile and eyes that give you away.

It's OK, we've all been there. This is what happens when we give children the power to determine our well-being, when we are on the back foot coping with a child instead of being on the front foot teaching them how to behave.

Seeing a top-notch meet and greet reminds me of the way cabin crew look and behave when I board a plane. Their dress code is uber-smart, immaculately coiffured, eyes bright, shoes and teeth sparkling; all of this providing subliminal reassurance that whoever tightened the wing nuts pays the same attention to detail. Receiving their full attention and beaming smiles, I cannot help but feel welcome, which relaxes me a little. All of this routine behaviour is designed to put us at our ease and thus to affect our behaviour in a positive manner. (I am talking from a UK perspective here; I am not thinking of the so-laid-back-we-might-fall-over regime I experienced a few years back when flying from Tampa to Cuba.)

Scan the classroom from the door while you meet and greet; make sure they go to their places according to your seating plan. This shows that you are the boss and that you are 'with it' – that is, aware of everything happening in the room. Have you seen *The Return of the Pink Panther*? Peter Sellers' hapless Inspector Clouseau arrests a blind beggar for some trivial misdemeanour, oblivious to the bank raid that is going on just yards away. This is a warning to us all: performing a proper meet and greet must be done with one eye on the classroom.

Your meet and greet is also an opportunity to gently challenge anyone who arrives in a giddy manner. Gently but firmly turn them around: 'Rahim, you seem a little het up. Take a moment, then try again, thank you.' This demonstrates your standards, and they will soon learn. What you accept, you establish. You can direct them to the work, repeating a mantra in-between the personal words that you have with some individuals, something like, 'Good morning everyone. Planners out – your starter is on the board, thank you.'

I sometimes see staff in schools standing mute at their classroom doors as the kids file past, and it is obvious: they are doing what they have been told to do but they have no idea why they are doing it. If only they knew that meet and greet, when it is done right, is 100% in their interests. Pupils arriving at school tomorrow morning will be, just like adults are, in myriad emotional states. Some will have been lovingly tucked into bed at a sensible hour with cocoa and a story, some will have been on the Xbox until 3am and, tragically, some will have spent hours listening to domestic violence. The football pundit, ex-England and Arsenal striker Ian Wright has spoken movingly on *Desert Island Discs* about his older brother, who would clamp his hands over young Ian's ears to protect him from the worst of the violence raging downstairs.[3]

Children who suffer like this see you and I, at least at first, as just more adults who will inevitably let them down. The meet and greet is your best chance to break this cycle, to show that you are not a threat, by communicating with the amygdala – the part of the brain that assigns emotional significance to events. Your consistently genuine smile and warm welcome will set off physiological changes, allowing that child to focus and, over time, will enable them to perceive you as something other than just another hostile adult.

Remember too that the other end of the lesson is just as important. A good 'end and send' is as important as your meet and greet. Get this right, and the pupils will leave your room with a clear understanding of what they have learned and a strong impression of a calm, ordered environment. Achieving this means careful timekeeping, so there is time to review today's learning, write down the homework, pack away calmly and leave in something approaching a civilised fashion.

---

3   *Desert Island Discs*, BBC Radio 4 (16 February 2020). Available at: https://www.bbc.co.uk/programmes/m000fdxw.

The whole-class welcome

Some lessons seem to start by stealth; pupils just arrive and get on with it. There are probably times when this is appropriate, but most often a whole-class welcome is a very good idea as it sets the tone. I am talking about the moment when you get everybody's attention, welcome them all and introduce today's lesson. You sound pleased to see the class, you refer back to last time to link the learning, you set out the aims and objectives for today and, quite possibly, you also share a little joke or two. The whole-class welcome establishes your authority, leads into the taking of the register and cues the class into following all your other established routines.

Routines and anxiety

Human beings in all cultures turn red when they are embarrassed. It is a shame that this link between emotional experience and temporary skin colour has not developed further. Imagine how much better teaching would be if children turned blue when they were bored? Seriously, if children experiencing anxiety turned green, we would have a much better picture of what is really going on in the room. We can be told, over and over, the percentage of children experiencing mental health problems (at time of writing, the excellent Nip in the Bud currently estimates that one person in five experiences a depressive episode before their eighteenth birthday[4]) and we know the pandemic has affected young people's well-being very badly, but it sure would help if we could *see* it.

Until that day, we need to be consistently welcoming, exuding personal warmth and seemingly genuinely pleased to see every last one of our pupils. They will be easier to teach if we do. And the more your lessons are governed by routines, the more children will know what is coming. They will know what is expected of them and their anxiety levels will drop. You can establish routines for getting equipment out, for tidying away (with or without the theme from *Mission Impossible* playing), for handing out books and collecting them back in, for getting into groups and for turning to partners. More routine leads to less anxiety which leads to better behaviour. QED.

---

4   See https://www.nipinthebud.org/fact-sheet/depression-in-children.

Have a plan

New teachers enter the profession these days with a mountain of assessment and self-assessment, planning, evaluation, monitoring and so on to do. They have plans for meeting every individual need, showing that every child has made progress every twenty minutes, picking up on who is underperforming, addressing various learning needs – I could go on. Yet, I still see well-intentioned, talented teachers who step into the ring without a plan for behaviour. Such a plan should cover:

▦ The precise behaviours you want to see.

▦ How you will tell the class about them.

▦ How you will highlight and reward excellent behaviour.

▦ The language you will use when correcting inappropriate behaviour.

▦ The consequences you are prepared to use.

As they say, PPPPP or proper planning prevents poor performance. I am told that the Australian men's cricket team use an extra P, and I will let you guess what it is. One of the chief purposes of the plan is to prevent those awful moments when you feel compelled to do *something*, but you do not know what, and then all kinds of foam and random words start spewing from your mouth: 'Right! That's it! I'm taking you to the head teacher and you can apologise to him right now!'

Now, there is a hostage to fortune that a little pre-planning and thinking time might have prevented.

The engager activity

It has been fashionable for some years now to put an activity on the board that pupils engage with as soon as they arrive; almost like flypaper that pupils will stick to instantly. A question or puzzle is good, such as displaying four images and asking which is the odd one out, or four extreme close-ups and asking what they might be. This tactic can work well, and its frequent success highlights an obvious point that sometimes gets missed: if you can hook children's natural curiosity then they will want to learn, and all talk of behaviour becomes irrelevant.

My only concern about the engager activity is that it can hamper the building of a relationship between class and teacher. Pupils arrive, are shown to their desks, look up at the board, pick up their pens and off they go. My question to staff is always, 'When do you come up for air? When do you build a sense of community?' My attitude was that Mr Baker's Year 10 English group was an exclusive club. I developed a special relationship with my GCSE classes; we had in-jokes and we had 'characters' (and I tried to make sure that every child was a character). We got the work done, of course, but we would stop now and then for a chat and a bit of a laugh. Life is short, and I wanted to share some of the joy of being alive with my classes. I am all for a purposeful start to lessons, so long as that relationship between teacher and taught, and the joy it can bring, is not squeezed out.

To sum up, if you can use the first five minutes of the lesson to demonstrate your high standards and your status as top dog in the room, you are well on your way to establishing a terrific working atmosphere.

Lesson structures that provoke curiosity

I was in a history lesson once, being taught by a fabulous (unqualified, at the time, as it happens) history teacher in a Leeds academy. She introduced the subject of evacuees, those children who were transported to the countryside from urban centres and other places of danger for their own protection during the Second World War. The class looked at a textbook and did one or two brief verbal and written activities. Then the teacher showed a video. It was the opening scene of a wartime drama: a distraught mother was waving her children off at a railway station. The class watched it politely but without any sign that it had particularly grabbed them.

Now, suppose that, instead of telling her class all about who the evacuees were and why they were travelling, that young teacher had shown them the video first. She would have been bombarded with questions: 'Why is that woman leaving her kids?' 'Where are they going?' and so on. Tweaking the lesson plan would have engaged their curiosity and learning would have happened at a faster pace.

It's getting loud in here!

At Ilford County High School, way back in the 1970s, our dinner times were supervised by Mrs Prue. What a name: a one-woman pupil referral unit! She wore a beehive do above horn-rimmed specs. While we all chatted away, as most humans do over a meal, Mrs Prue would continually bang a metal spoon on the nearest table yelling 'Be quiet!' though her East End accent and the room's cavernous acoustics reduced this to 'Bay choir!'

The dinner hall was a separate building some distance from any other; it seemed to me that no one else could possibly be bothered by the noise, so why did Mrs Prue not just jack it in and leave us alone? If you would like less noise in your classroom, assuming you do not carry a metal spoon and you want more success than Mrs Prue achieved, you might think about establishing a routine.

The easiest one is to define, set and rehearse noise levels, perhaps 'one-to-one voice' for talking to the person next to you, 'group voice' for conversation around a table and 'room voice' for whole-class contributions. This use of shorthand is very effective. With younger children, you might like to cover all learning needs when you introduce a routine like this, so that they hear it, see it and do it.

I have had great success helping teachers with noise with the simplest of suggestions. I have mentioned it already several times: a 'one voice' rule. Put simply, there should be one voice audible at any given moment, unless there is pair or group discussion going on. With persistence, 'one voice' becomes a memorable, accepted routine.

Establish a signal for attention

Do you own a dog? I will not ask about cats, as they are famously immune to commands, but the dog owners among you will have a word or phrase that you use to elicit civilised behaviour from your pooch. Let me guess: it is probably 'Sit'. When you want your dog to stop, be quiet and wait for your next command, you say 'Sit' with a firm but friendly tone, yes? Now, imagine trying it this way: 'Rex? ... Ahem! ... Sit down for me, will you ... I'm waiting

... Rex? ... Please ... I won't tell you again ... Come on, it's your time you are wasting ...' How successful would that be? No, not very.

You need to establish a signal that pupils will learn to respond to. If they hear you give five different signals for quiet in rapid succession, they will wait to hear what six, seven and eight sound like before they think about complying. Primary staff are brilliant at this. They use simple phrases like '1, 2, 3, eyes on me!' or they clap in rhythmic patterns that their classes must copy. Some use a countdown. This was always my favourite signal for attention: 'I need quiet Year 8 on 3 ... looking this way ... 2, pens down ... 1, everyone listening ... And ... stop!'

Interleaving the numbers with a description of exactly what you want helps to gather them all together. Speak slowly, with an optimistic tone of voice as if you genuinely expect compliance from everyone. I have seen staff fall into a number of traps when attempting to use the countdown:

- They fire the numbers at the class like bullets: '3! ... 2! ... 1!' This aggressive delivery betrays anxiety which does not encourage cooperation.

- They start counting down while hunting for something in a desk drawer. If you are distracted, why would anyone pay attention to you?

- They interrupt the countdown: '3, looking this way ... Isaac put that down. Oh, and Jeremy, are you sandwiches or school dinner today? ... 2, pens down ...' and so on. The effect is ruined.

- They see 80% of the class comply and they think, 'That will do.' This is a big mistake; if you accept 20% of the class ignoring the instruction on day one, it will be 60% by the end of the week.

- They count upwards: '1 ... 2 ... 3' after which some wag shouts '4' and jovial chaos ensues.

- They omit 'stop', announcing '3 ... 2 ... 1' to which another wag adds 'Blast off!' and here we go again.

It is important to describe exactly what behaviour you need by 'stop'. Give them as much information as you can about what you want them to do – and *keep* giving!

Other signals are available, naturally. Some staff raise an arm in the air, for example. I find this works best when pupils are expected to do the same and, as I said earlier, if you wait until everyone is doing it. I say 'everyone' but if Robin is sitting on his hands, you can address this and move on: 'Thank you, everyone. (Quietly) Robin, I'll speak to you later ... Now, turn to page 8 ...'

A signal for gaining *your* attention

How do pupils get *your* attention? I wish I had a quid for every time I have seen a teacher say, 'Hands up to speak, thank you,' and within two minutes they have answered a shouted-out question. They may as well paint the classroom wall with letters two feet high that say: 'DON'T LISTEN TO ME. I DON'T MEAN ANYTHING I SAY!' As soon as you answer a shouted comment you have given that behaviour the green light, and your 'raise a hand' rule is toast.

If your routine is 'hands up', stick to it. As a rule, do not answer anyone who calls out, except to correct their behaviour; and if Aneela at the back, who never speaks in your lesson, forswears her vow of silence and shouts out an answer or a question one day that you simply cannot bear to ignore, reinforce your rule once she has said her piece: 'Thank you, Aneela. Hand up next time, remember!'

Resist at all costs the temptation to call out instructions over the general hubbub. If you call out, so will they. If you talk while they do, you are accepting the noise.

Can you see my body talk?

As I said earlier, children can sniff uncertainty a mile off. Getting your body language right is vital. Remember, 80% of what you communicate is non-verbal.[5] Find a strong position in the room and stand there. Still and straight. The class is a pack and you are the leader. If you dash about the place, you will not seem to be relaxed, and if you do not seem relaxed, you are not in charge, are you?

Make deliberate use of your hands – or at least decide what they will be doing. It is amazing how enormous your hands can seem when you don't know where to put them. Establish eye contact with as many pupils as possible. Think about your clothes too. I have seen staff with scruffy shoes, visible underwear and many other crimes against common sense. Scruffy shoes tell the world that you do not respect yourself, and if I have to explain to a teacher why visible underwear is not appropriate, well, they are in the wrong job. Speak as quietly as you can get away with. If your voice is too loud, you give the impression that you expect a noisy class.

Whole-school routines

Every school has its little quirks. For example, you might teach in a school where pupils are expected to stand up behind their chairs at the start of the lesson, before you give them the nod to sit down. You might think this is daft, but even if you do, I advise you to go along with it. When a new teacher arrives and airily dismisses one of the whole-school expectations, her classes will assume that all bets are off and anything goes.

You might find you have to operate the dreaded C1, C2, C3 system. My advice, until you are established enough to promote alternatives, is to use it – but do not rely on it. Place greater emphasis on relationships, respect and routines. Remind children of your expectations constantly, and catch them being good relentlessly. In other words, you may need to use the C system, but it should not be your only response to behaviour.

---

5   James O'Sullivan, 80% Of All Communication is Non-Verbal, *Leap29* (27 May 2016). Available at: https://www.leap29.com/blog/80-of-all-communication-is-no-verbal.

Some routines really need to be applied whole school as standard operating procedures, or 'SOPs'. Latecomers are a good example. Jake turns up late to period one for Mr Jones, who loudly demands to know why he is late and angrily tells him to take a seat. He turns up late to period two for Miss Henshall, who makes him wait outside the room until she is ready to have a private word with him. He turns up late for Mr Brown, who calmly indicates an empty chair and says, 'Good morning, Jake. I'll speak with you in a moment.' You can tell which one I prefer. It is not, as they say, rocket science.

Equipment is another one. Laura goes to maths without a pen; Mr Hardcastle gives her a stern lecture. She goes to English without a pen; Miss Cooper hands her a pen without comment. She goes to technology without a pen; Mr Hibberd sells her a pen. Laura gleans the impression that Mr Hardcastle is nasty, Miss Cooper is nice and Mr Hibberd is just a bit weird. You can argue for consistency in staff meetings, but right now you will just have to choose your own routine and stick to it. At least Jake and Laura will know what to expect from you.

Beware routines

I once watched a reception teacher in Manchester. I am a huge fan of primary teachers, and I have seen some exceptional practice all over the country. Sadly, this was not one of those days. The class were on the mat in front of the teacher singing the class song. She was modelling the actions that went with it – something like, 'We are caring, we are kind, we keep everyone in mind!' The actions involved pointing to oneself and others ('We'), holding both hands tight against the place where a heart should be ('Caring') and tracing a huge circle in the air ('Everyone.') Can you imagine a teacher performing this song and its accompanying actions with a bored-sick expression and floppy, lifeless hands? That was her. It would have been funny if it had not meant that these children were getting a raw deal. I tell that story now to say that routine is a double-edged sword. It must not become staid, and it cannot be allowed to stifle passion and spontaneity.

Having a routine means having a plan. Whether it is Year 1 making their lunch choices or Year 11 gathering at the front of the lab to watch you dissect a mouse, if you have established a routine, this means that you have decided exactly how pupils should behave. You have rehearsed these behaviours with them and you have persistently acknowledged those who follow the routine. Great content and delivery can go a long way towards making pupil engagement automatic. Established routines provide the structure that keeps your pupils on track when they might otherwise stray.

Takeaways

▨ Taking an accurate register is the most important part of your lessons.

▨ If the first five minutes of your lessons are governed by solid routines, you are on the road to success.

▨ Establishing how you will gain pupils' attention and how they will gain yours is one of the most effective actions you can take to reduce low-level disruption.

▨ Building a sense of community is vital, so ensure that your routines support this.

▨ If you can hook pupils' curiosity, they will want to learn and behaviour will become irrelevant.

NOW TRY THIS:

Look at Appendix 5. How well established are these basic routines in your teaching? What actions are you prompted to take?

Look through your timetable for the week. Where are the stress points when your organisation can come under strain? How might you plan to overcome these challenges?

Chapter 5

RELATIONSHIPS

Well, maybe teaching is a relationship-based activity, I hear you say, but my classes are tearing me apart. How on earth am I supposed to build relationships? The answer is to play a long game. With patience and courage, armed by your conviction that you are the adult, that children are people and that behaviour can be taught, you will begin to build bridges.

Why relationships matter

I watched a maths teacher recently, Mr D, in the North East of England. He had a small Year 9 class, maybe fifteen to twenty pupils, and they were giving him a hard time. He was calm, respectful and used a lot of positive scripts, but it got him nowhere. Half the class sat mute and motionless. The other half sniggered behind their hands and made silly comments across the room. Some roamed about. Still, he soldiered on, focusing on the maths, choosing pupils to help him with the algebra example that was on the whiteboard and tactically ignoring quite a lot.

Mr D persevered with his positive scripts – 'I need you to listen', 'Looking this way, thank you' – and used a calm, respectful tone, but he may as well not have been there. It was as if a glass screen separated him from the class. I sat back in my chair and thought about it. What was going wrong here? He would doubtless tell me when we met for the feedback that he was doing all the positive stuff, and I could not disagree, so why was it not working? What would I say to him? Then it hit me: he was using respectful scripts in a doomed attempt to control the children, rather than using them because showing respect was the correct thing to do.

I met with Mr D later that day. After praising his perseverance and use of positive scripts, I came out with it: 'Do you have a relationship with that class?' He had been doing all the right things, but only in the same sense that Eric Morecambe played all the right notes (that is an old-timer's cultural reference; look it up on YouTube if you need to – you will not be sorry). I told him that spouting respectful language was not enough. He needed to look like he wanted to be there. He needed to get to know his pupils and to connect with each one individually. I described how this would lead to a positive atmosphere in which he and the class would thrive together. I could feel his scepticism, but later that same day, when I delivered behaviour CPD to the staff in the school hall, I was pleased to see Mr D sitting up-front and taking notes.

I went back a month later. What a difference! I was shown to Mr D's classroom where I found him teaching the same group, and I must say his obvious progress made me quite emotional. The stony face was gone, replaced with a smile and regular laughter. The catcalls and the roaming about had ceased. The class were quiet and focused. Mr D told me later that he had experienced a moment of clarity. The kids were people, and he needed to talk *to* them rather than *at* them. The deputy principal told me later how she had seen him out and about on the corridor, getting to know the kids and discussing the woes of Sunderland United, among other subjects.

I was overjoyed to see the benefits writ large in the classroom. Mr D had changed and so had his pupils. When I asked him about all this, he was kind enough to thank me, and then he smiled: 'I'm much more authentic now.' Realisation had dawned. Positive scripts are not magic spells; they are examples of the language people use when they respect one another. Once Mr D realised this, he became a more genuine, relatable and happy teacher.

Building relationships

The English language is full of metaphors that have become so familiar that they almost disappear. 'Building relationships' is a good example. Having renovated holiday lets, I have some recent experience to call upon. So, let us go with the idea that in developing relationships with pupils and classes, you are building (verb) a building (noun), and see where it gets us.

The first question for any builder is, what is the purpose of the structure in question? If your building does not have a clear purpose, then you will end up with a compromised edifice that you cannot use, rent or sell. Anyone involved in the Millennium Dome fiasco will tell you that. So, what is the purpose of this relationship we are building? If it is purely to 'get the buggers to shut up', then you are unlikely to succeed. That is where Mr D was at. However, it is true to say that once you have established a working relationship with your charges, they are more likely to let you get on with your lesson. More importantly, once a relationship has been established, you will be able to take risks, as pupils will give you the benefit of the doubt when you need to tackle an off-putting topic or activity. In other words, they will trust you – a bit like a horse that has been broken in – and all this will benefit learning.

Working with young people can be tremendous fun. I used to look forward to my GCSE classes with great anticipation. However, if enjoying their company should ever unmoor itself from facilitating their learning, you will be off-piste, and all those issues about boundaries might rear their heads. If your good humour becomes self-indulgent, you are in for trouble, as your pupils will soon see through the 'funny' teacher who is simply amusing himself.

A building needs good foundations. In my classroom, these included:

- Respect for the children as people.

- Respect towards me – on the basis that I worked hard to earn and retain it.

- One voice at a time.

- Promises kept, good and bad.

- Calm, quiet entry to the room.

- Basic routines governing most activities (movement, homework collection, taking the register and so on).

- Making the learning as relevant and enjoyable as I could.

- To borrow Bill Rogers' phrases, 'positive reinforcement' of desired behaviour and 'positive correction' of undesired behaviour.[1]

It is worth noting that the experience of the building (verb) is part of the purpose of the building (noun). It took my partner Sian and I five years to

1   Bill Rogers, *Behaviour Management: A Whole-School Approach* (London: SAGE, 2007), p. 51.

renovate our outbuildings. It was backbreaking, exhilarating, painful, hilarious, boring and surprising all at the same time (rather like teaching, I hear you say). We share special memories of wet days spent mucking out the gutters with our numb, frozen fingers or shovelling gravel into the cement mixer for hours on end. Despite enduring this physical torture, many people go on and on, doing up properties, selling and starting again. Quite apart from the obvious financial rewards, I see why they do it: the process has become its own outcome.

Life is short and the process of getting there is as important as one's arrival, which is why celebrities often report feeling empty and dissatisfied when they achieve all they have ever wanted in their early twenties. The striving is as important as the outcome. Your relationships with pupils are the same. You will cry, laugh and from time to time you will bang your head on the table in frustration before they leave your care, and even then they will not be the finished article. But being a part of their formative years is a special privilege that 99% of the public do not have, and we do well to remember that.

A building needs a plan. Planning to build a relationship is a good start to make when you are faced with Declan, who has a monobrow, breathes fire and tells you your subject is 'shit'. If, instead of thinking, 'How will I cope with/overcome/squash this troublemaker?' you approach him with, 'How will I build a relationship with this young person?' you are on the right track. I would be lying if I said halfway there, but definitely in the right and most effective direction. The key will be Declan seeing you as part of his solution and not part of his problem.

Your friendly meet and greet will help. You can speak to Declan's amygdala way before his conscious mind realises what you are up to. You are not a threat. That is the message. Pointed fingers, furrowed brows and raised voices are out. A genuine welcome and, when necessary, calm statements of fact about the rules, about his behaviour and about where we go next, are in. You may meet more resistance than you can possibly imagine, and you will not be the first to have tried, but your refusal to rise to his snarky, cutting remarks and your refusal to bear grudges will work wonders. When a sanction is necessary, choosing to hold a restorative chat with Declan rather than sitting him in a silent detention will also help.

The emotional bank account

In his book, *The 7 Habits of Highly Effective People*, Stephen Covey writes about the Emotional Bank Account.[2] In a classroom it works like this. When you welcome the class, when you ask Jane about her mum who is in hospital, when you have a quick word with Tom about the weekend's football, and when you hand Ellie a cutting you took from the newspaper about a ballet you thought she might be interested in, you are making deposits in the emotional bank accounts that each of those children has with you.

This drip-drip-drip of emotional investment will mean that when you get it wrong, and you pay out from the account, you will still be in credit. We all have bad days. Maybe you row with your partner before you leave the house, and your car breaks down on the way to school, and then you find out you have been overlooked for that second-in-department role you had your heart set on, and you just about keep it together until some poor child rolls her eyes at you. Boom! You snap at her, and this counts as a withdrawal. But you have been paying in, day in, day out, and so this child knows that you care and is willing to understand that miss is not her best self today and will not hate you forever.

Tragically, there are some adults working in our schools who do not understand the need to make the payments, and they are the ones who constantly cry out for bigger and more punitive sanctions. Relationships are out of the question for these poor souls, and they waste their time moaning that 'something should be done' when the thing that needed doing was in their power to do. I would contrast them with the vast armies of teaching assistants, learning mentors and other colleagues who take an interest in Minecraft, Pokémon and World Wrestling Entertainment Top Trumps, not because these things float their boats but because their pupils love them, and they know that showing an interest in *their* interests is the way to form an attachment and a strong productive relationship.

---

2   Stephen R. Covey, *The 7 Habits of Highly Effective People: Powerful Lessons in Personal Change* (New York: Simon & Schuster, 2017).

Boundaries

Back at Ilford County High in the 1970s, a supply teacher arrived from Australia: a Mr Schaedel. One morning break, to our utter disbelief, my mate Chris and I saw him on the school field. He was not strolling around on duty, coffee in hand; he was joining in with a game of football! We rubbed our eyes and looked a second time; yes, it really was happening. Amid the many games that raged on the field one of them stood out a mile, featuring twenty or so grammar school boys in their maroon blazers and one blond grown-up bloke in an anorak and Farahs. We could not have been more amazed if he had stripped naked and stood on the school roof, waving a bottle of brandy and singing 'Funiculì Funiculà'.

No doubt Mr Schaedel had the best of intentions, but it was like watching a Dalek necking a cold beer and tapas with the Doctor in the TARDIS. This. Does. Not. Happen. We weren't in the least impressed by his man-of-the-people stance; we just thought he had lost his mind, and we wondered how long it would be before he was carpeted in the head teacher's office. (It happened later the same day, if I remember correctly.) Your school is unlikely to be as repressive as mine was, but all the same, you will need to keep in mind that there are limitations to what you can or should do with pupils.

Too much information

You will have been told many times to 'get to know your pupils', and this is excellent advice, but how far should they get to know you? A bit of self-disclosure is helpful; it humanises you. And, after all, if you are asking them to share, then you need to share too. But, as with social media, everything you share is out there for good and cannot be retrieved, so you will need to think carefully about what you reveal.

Good sharing	Bad sharing
▤ Where were you born?	▤ Where were you on Saturday night?
▤ How many siblings do you have?	▤ How many pints can you drink?
▤ What made you teach your subject?	▤ What made you choose that dress?
▤ Do you have a favourite author?	▤ Do you have a boyfriend?

Pupils know that teachers love to talk, so beware the innocent question asked by the front row, like, 'How's the baby, sir?' or, 'Did you see the West Ham game, miss?' Five minutes later, you will realise you have been had, that the little sods fancied some downtime and that tricking you into an irrelevant conversation was the easiest way to get it. A personable, 'She's lovely, thanks! How are you getting on with question two?' is probably a good way to respond. In the case of West Ham, my answer was usually, 'Thanks for asking but it's too painful to talk about. How are you getting on with question two?' I only wish they were asking now when the Hammers are playing so much better. Since David Moyes became manager we have really begun to … oops. You see? There I go again …

The dreaded 'crush'

Let us get this out of the way: if a pupil does anything that suggests they have any kind of crush on you, you need to report it *immediately*. For a week or two, during my first year of teaching, a very long time ago, a Year 11 girl kept turning up at my classroom door at the end of the day. I would humour her for a bit and then say something like, 'I really need to be getting on.' But she kept doing this day after day, until I lost patience one afternoon and, seeing her approach, I loudly cried, 'For God's sake!' She burst into tears, thrust a package into my hands and ran off, never to be seen again.

It was a pint glass with my name on it. I felt awful for hurting the poor girl's feelings but, in fact, I should have been firmer from the start. On her second appearance, I should have explained gently but plainly that her behaviour was not appropriate, or at the very least I should have spoken to her form teacher and asked them to put the girl straight.

If something like this happens to you, write down everything that takes place, with dates, times and locations, and make sure your designated safeguarding lead knows. Never be alone with a child and make sure you are always visible to passers-by. Hormonal changes can do strange things to adolescents. They are learning about relationships and experimenting with new roles, and they can struggle to separate fiction from reality. Your arrival as a young, relatable figure can set off all sorts of confusing feelings in a teenage mind, so you are doing your pupils a favour when you draw a very clear line.

Think about what you wear too. A deputy head teacher I knew had to send several young female staff home some years ago because their thongs were visible above low-waisted jeans. I would be the last to blame women for men's reaction to what they wear, but in a school you do not need to have watched *The Inbetweeners* to know that some discretion is advisable. For the sake of balance, this is also my chance to ask any male PE teachers out there, do you really need to wear shorts when teaching geography? (Just kidding.)

Favourites

It is very easy to have favourites whether you mean to or not. After all, there are some pupils whose company you look forward to and some you do not. Some are punctual, work hard, know when to have a laugh with you and when to get back to work. They have personality, wit and style. Others are just a tad less appealing. Maybe they shout out, argue back, mess about or perhaps they just sit mute. Will they receive the same deal from you? Of course they will, you might say to me, but consider this: you may not feel threatened when D'arcy speaks out of turn, but when Dylan does it, how does that feel? This is the root of much unfairness in the classroom, and it is your amygdala making bad decisions for you. You absolutely must be fair.

I was watching a Year 5 primary lesson in Scotland and the teacher, who happened to be the deputy head, was demonstrating long division on the board. He chose an angelic little girl, resembling the child on the famous Pears Soap advert, to take him through the various stages of the sum and, as she announced each separate calculation, he recorded it on the board. When the correct answer was found, Miss Pears received a Golden Star. Meanwhile, on his own at the back of the classroom, sat Eddie, who was there to give his regular teacher some respite. Eddie suffered fits of violent temper and one such incident had occurred the previous day. When the deputy began the next sum, Eddie's hand went up, and Eddie performed exactly as his angelic predecessor had done, until the sum was complete. Do you think Eddie received a Golden Star? Of course not. Eddie was notorious for his poor behaviour, but this golden opportunity to make him feel valued and important for the most positive of reasons was entirely missed.

I used to give my pupils a questionnaire in the first lesson, asking them subject stuff like, 'What was your favourite topic last year?' and also some personal things like pets, hobbies, memorable moments and so on. They appreciated my curiosity, and their answers gave me something I could tag them with. In the weeks and months that followed, I could enquire about the well-being of the hamster or gently tease them about being rescued from the freezer when they were 2 years old, or whatever the story was. It is important that every child is a celebrity in your classroom, not just one or two. Also, it is important to stay curious. When couples fall out of love, it often means they have stopped being curious about each other. They look at one another and assume they know all there is to know. Be curious about your pupils, and stay that way if you can. This will make your restorative chats more meaningful for both parties.

Mine, permanent and safe

Back in 2003, I become a behaviour and attendance consultant for Wakefield local authority. As this was a national initiative, all new consultants in Yorkshire and the Humber were given six days of training at the York Hilton, led by the splendid Judith Harwood and assisted by the equally splendid Mike O'Connor. In that brief period, they taught me more than I can put in one book, but something Mike told me has stayed with me above all the rest. 'There are three things a child wants to know in any classroom,' he said. 'Is it mine? Is it permanent? Is it safe?'

Is it mine?

When the child is wondering, 'Is it mine?' they are asking, is this going to help me in some way? Do I at least recognise its relevance?

You might already have been challenged with, 'When am I ever going to need to know about algebra/sonnets/French verbs/anticyclones?' If you can start where your pupils are you have a fighting chance, but the world is changing fast and appearing relevant can be tough. For example, the chances are that you and I, dear reader, differ widely in what information we consume and how. I have a large CD collection and I get my news from BBC Radio 4. Assuming most of you reading this are in your twenties, there is a good chance that you occupy a very different cultural space to me.

We probably use differing vocabularies too. My grown-up kids keep me on the straight and narrow. I used the word 'moist' recently in an entirely innocent context and they both nearly threw up. I once used the word 'romp' with a Year 7 class who, to my complete consternation, became hysterical. I think the Sunday red-tops have effectively redefined the word, and if you do not know what a red-top is then you are making my point for me. I digress, but only to underline that, youthful as you are, you will need to work harder than you think in order to demonstrate the relevance of your subject.

Working in close quarters with young people is a double-edged sword; it keeps you young but it also forces you to be prematurely old. At least twenty years ago, I mentioned Kiefer Sutherland. A boy called Jarred said, 'That's a blast from the past.' I said, 'No, not Donald Sutherland, *Kiefer*.' He looked confused and said, 'Yeah, I know!' We must make sure that the content we provide has relevance to our pupils' experience or they will think that our values of care, respect and common decency are irrelevant to them too.

Some staff miss obvious opportunities to make a connection. I was in Leeds not long ago working with a secondary maths teacher. A world-famous boy band were playing the First Direct Arena that very night. It might have been JLS or the Old Kids on the Block; I do not remember, as the prospect failed to excite me as much as it did Year 8. A maths teacher was busy failing to interest his pupils in how to work out the volume of a box. They fidgeted, they whispered and they looked out of the window, as bored children will. If only he had asked them to calculate the volume of the box-shaped stage on which the band would be cavorting that same evening a few miles away,

I think he might have caught their imagination. Instead, the lesson took place entirely on far-off Planet Maths, some eight trillion light years from the experience of a 12-year-old from Burmantofts. There are other distant bodies, like Planet French and Planet Poetry, on which similar staff remain, marooned for all time, unable to capture a single young person to share their grisly fate.

Is it permanent?

If you have taught for more than a term, you will have noticed that when you reappeared after the holiday there was a slight frisson as the pupils registered your continuing presence. You will have noticed too that behaviour was slightly better. By turning up you had become more trustworthy. And it is all about trust. Pupils are dying to hang a medal around your neck that says, 'Reliable adult', and by coming back for more you are a little nearer the podium. We all know the ordeal that supply teachers face, which is why so many schools have appointed cover supervisors. Kids behave rather better for staff they know. Not perfectly, as any cover supervisor will tell you, but better, by and large. A supply teacher is by definition here today, gone tomorrow and so less trustworthy and also less able to apply any kind of consequence. Some excellent schools find ways to ensure that poor behaviour for supply staff is followed up, but in my experience they are in the minority.

There is also an emotional aspect to permanence. You are not leaving. Not only will you be there for the child today, tomorrow, next week and next term, but also you cannot be driven away. We have all heard the harrowing stories of foster families who endure the most appalling behaviour from children when they first arrive in the home, and often for a good while after. These young people have been let down by their primary carers and they are terrified that every adult will do the same. So, what do they do? They test out the new adults. They put their new carers through hell, again and again, until they finally accept that the new regime can be trusted.

Pupils in school are frequently acting out in the same manner. You are just another adult who will reject them at the first sign of trouble, or so they think. Part of providing permanence is repeating this message, explicitly and implicitly: 'I'm not going anywhere, and I'm not giving up on you.' I first heard this phrase when Paul Dix used it in a training session that I was lucky enough to attend, and I seized on it because it articulated something that had always been implicit in my approach. During my time as a head of year, I was described by some as a 'maverick'; I suppose I was dabbling in relational practice without knowing there was a word for it. Establishing relational practice in a school means making the maverick the mainstream by being explicit about our values.

If a pupil stubbornly refuses to engage then that is their choice, but you are not going anywhere; you will not give up but will remain open to them changing their mind. Before COVID-19, some very wise teachers used to shake hands with their pupils at the classroom door. Occasionally, pupils would refuse, but that hand of friendship would still be available the next day, and the next, and the next. It may be a while before we are all comfortable once more to shake hands with learners, but that metaphorical hand of friendship can remain outstretched; there are other ways to offer a genuine welcome and a fresh start every day.

Is it safe?

It might be hard to accept, but you are one of the biggest potential threats to classroom safety, if not the biggest. I quoted Haim Ginott in Chapter 1 discussing 'tools of torture', and sarcasm is one of the sharpest. When I was doing press-ups one day, my PE teacher, sick of seeing me fail to ground my nose, did so by treading on my head, making my nose bleed – a single moment that perfectly sums up my secondary education. But this was nowhere near as damaging as my biology teacher, Mr Snook, who stood behind his raised desk and sneered at my approaching 14-year-old self: 'Ah, Baker – what snivelling excuse have you got for me this week?' And this guy was in charge of the Christian Union!

I could not explain my disengagement. I could not tell him that the smell of the lab repelled me or that I found all the long words on the board completely intimidating. As a grammar school boy I was supposed to understand them, after all. I just stood and weathered his destructive 'humour'. He should have been called Mr Snark. If I tell you never to be sarcastic, a lightning bolt will shoot from the sky and destroy my laptop because I am sure I sinned in this manner on occasion, certainly in my first year or two while I was flailing around and self-knowledge was a pipe dream. But, for most of my career, this behaviour reared its head only in friendly banter with pupils who knew me, who knew I cared about them and their progress, and who had a relationship with me that was secure enough to take it. In its rawest form, sarcasm is the most destructive behaviour in which you can indulge. If praise is the basil in the classroom, which you can sprinkle about liberally (but not blindly), sarcasm is the asafoetida – a pungent spice that needs very careful handling.

I do not suppose Mr Snook realised what a delicate flower I was; he just saw an immature fellow whose imaginary dog kept eating his homework, but I remember that moment from 1976 like it was yesterday – and not because it did anything to bolster my resolve, self-respect or love for biology. Every pupil needs to know they are safe in your room, safe from your sarcasm and safe from being thumped by the school bully while you turn your back or dive into the stockroom. Imagine that kid who has been awake half the night listening to dad assaulting mum. What kind of classroom does he need?

In Sheffield schools, back in the day, the word 'gay' was used as an all-purpose word for anything that was weak, dumb or otherwise unacceptable. One morning, Gary, one of my Year 10s, apropos of nothing, set off on quite a soliloquy: 'I hate p***s, I hate q***s, I hate gay bastards' and so on. I quickly intervened, with calm palms aloft, hoping to educate rather than condemn: 'Gary, Gary! You seem to assume that there are no gay people in the room.' He sat bolt upright and scanned the classroom like a sweaty, overweight meerkat. I suppose he was looking for the odd one out. Then his gaze settled on me: 'Is it you, sir? Are you gay?'

I now know that you should not answer questions of this sort, since doing so may encourage the outing of gay colleagues, but way back then I knew no different, and so I replied, 'No, Gary. I'm heterosexual.' His verdict was thunderous: 'That's *nearly* as *bad*!'

I resolved to do something about this, so whenever I heard the word 'gay' used in a pejorative context, I would stop the lesson and deliver my little speech about what must it be like to come to school and hearing this word, which you are beginning to identify with, used constantly as an insult. It went on for a good five minutes. Pretty soon my classes became tired of hearing this homily and homophobic language was strangled at birth. Instead of, 'Shut up, you gay!' I heard, 'Shut up you g … g … g … Oh, never mind.'

Years later, Nick, one of the boys in that class, and now a college pupil, came back to school to see me. We sat in my office where he told me, over a cup of tea, that he was gay, and he thanked me for making a safe space for him. One of my proudest moments in the job.

Children need to be kept safe from Tall Poppy Syndrome too. They need to feel free to take risks, to answer questions and, more importantly, to ask great questions. If someone on the back row mutters 'Wanker', they will soon stop taking the risk. Some pupils look askance at any peer who conspicuously tries to excel and take great joy in cutting them off at the knees. This is a form of revenge taken by pupils who are hurting in some way, and one of the four goals of misbehaviour, as identified by Austrian psychiatrist Rudolf Dreikurs, which we will look at more closely in Chapter 9. I wonder if this mechanism was at work when my fellow Year 6 pupil, Tony Sherwood, heard me identify the music being played to the class as the 'Dance of the Sugar Plum Fairy'. He took great pleasure in informing his cronies, and so I was renamed 'The Sugar Plum Fairy' for the rest of the week. Deep joy.

This relates to bullying, of course, which could be another book in itself. To ensure bullying does not take root in your classroom, make sure you establish what behaviour you do want to see. Spend time and effort establishing your learning space as a put-down free zone. Always tackle and refuse to accept any kind of personal attacks. Everyone must leave the room at least as happy as they were when they entered it; that was my motto.

Keeping promises

It is important to keep your promises. You are building trust. Declan has no reason whatsoever to trust adults. Everyone he has ever met has let him down. Dad left the moment mum got pregnant, and he reappears every now and then making big promises that he never delivers. Mum tries hard but she is preoccupied with the baby she has had with her new partner, who is not overjoyed that Declan exists. How resentful, how hurt and how full of a burning desire for revenge on the world might you have been if you were in Declan's shoes? And yet your colleagues want to write him off as a 'bad kid'? Get alongside. Listen. Find out. Empathise ('I'm glad you told me') but do not sympathise ('You poor thing').

Whether it is a reward of some kind or five minutes at break for a restorative chat, if you have said it will happen, you absolutely *must* follow through. Anything that destroys trust will destroy the relationship. Declan has to know that no matter how badly he behaves, tomorrow is another day, and you will be there with a smile and a warm welcome. He might eventually begin to believe he deserves it, and until he does life will be rocky, but you are building to a plan, being your best self and also being probably the most effective and positive factor in Declan's young life.

This stuff can be learned

For some of you, all this relationship stuff is second nature. You are people persons, and although there is a lot to take in, it is basically how you roll, so you may be feeling quite chipper. However, some of you reading this book might be saying to yourselves, 'Help! I am not a people person. I want to teach __ (insert name of subject; I am going to avoid the temptation to stereotype any subjects by naming them here), but I am quite reserved, and all this talk of relationships has me in a cold sweat.'

If that is you, no problem. Just start by being aware that, as we saw in Chapter 3, learners' interpersonal abilities will be as crucial as their qualifications in the jobs market of the future. You may not be a people person, and that is OK. However, you may know someone who is, someone who always seems to get chatting with those they meet, such as taxi drivers, shop assistants and so on. Watch them. Observe how they do it. This is something you can practise. There is nothing to lose, and you may find that you begin to enjoy that passing human connection.

The excellent School of Life group has posted a wonderful video about relationships on YouTube.[3] It addresses relationships between partners and sets out three essential ingredients: kindness, understanding and shared vulnerability. I hope that elsewhere in this book I have already given you the impression that kindness and understanding matter. It is time for me to discuss shared vulnerability using a story about Alison, to whom I referred in Chapter 2.

In my first week of teaching, thirty-six years ago, Alison called me 'Spotty!' She was a 14-year-old with spikey hair and a spikey personality. Alison

---

3   See https://www.youtube.com/watch?v=UOn9HVQdOGc.

would have made a great character on *Coronation Street* – a tough woman, almost flinty, with steely blue eyes. Anyway, when I corrected her in some way, she shot around and spat, 'Arright, Sss-potty!'

At lunchtime, I told a colleague, who gave me some excellent advice. 'There's a vulnerable little girl inside that suit of armour; talk to *her.*' So, I sat down with Alison in the drama room at the end of the day, reminded myself that those steely blue eyes were but a mask, and launched in, telling her that this was my first week in the job, and although I was enjoying it immensely, it was pretty stressful and so I had a few more spots than normal. I can vividly remember those piercing eyes surveying me, as if through the slit in a medieval knight's helmet. It did not feel like a breakthrough moment at the time, but day by day, week by week, I found it easier to coexist with Alison, and my moment of shared vulnerability was at the root of this improvement. We need to show that we are human, if we want to be trusted.

To sum up, relationships take time to build, so take a long-term approach. If you do not receive the response you hope for immediately, do not snatch away the hand of friendship that you have extended. This is about building trust, and each individual will bring their own experiences to bear, affecting the speed at which that building progresses. Keep paying into those emotional bank accounts and the rewards will come.

Takeaways

- Make regular deposits in your emotional bank account with each child.

- Focus on keeping your pupils emotionally and physically safe. This will help them to achieve their potential.

- Avoid having favourites at all costs. Favouritism is insidious, so be self-aware and vigilant.

- Always keep your promises. Trust is at the heart of good relationships.

- Find ways to have fun. Do not let curriculum and other pressures crowd out having fun with young people.

NOW TRY THIS:

Consider your boundaries. How much do pupils know about you? Do they know how far they can go when interacting with you?

Next week, note down all the deposits you make into pupils' bank accounts. Do you notice any new opportunities? How does making these deposits affect your relationships with the pupils concerned?

Chapter 6

EXPECTATIONS

In this chapter, I hope to help you bridge the gap between the behaviour you would like to see and the behaviour you are experiencing. For many teachers, this means reaching a whole new level of clarity. What exactly do you expect? How will your pupils know?

Also, when it comes to teaching behaviour, there are those pupils – those with attachment issues and those experiencing a range of other difficulties – whose relationship with you, and whose experience of your behaviour, will determine how they respond to you far more than your routines, expectations and other aspects of teaching behaviour. I have devoted a chapter each to relationships (Chapter 5) and modelling (Chapter 7) for that very reason. In this chapter, I am mostly concerned with the general mass of your pupils.

What do you mean I cannot blame the kids?

Another lesson, early in my career, and another penny dropped. My Year 9 drama class were rioting. I suppose that is a slight exaggeration; it would be more accurate to say that they were making a great deal of noise, way off task and cheerfully ignoring my every word. It *felt* like a riot because I was supposed to be in charge, but in fact I was helpless. The situation swirled and spiralled like the nightmare scenario that began this book. My efforts to get quiet became more and more desperate, the room grew louder and louder, until finally I could stand it no longer and I threw in the towel. I walked out of the room, down the corridor, into the smokers' staffroom and lit a cigarette. And I do not even smoke.

My colleague John found me – close to tears, drowning in tobacco and self-loathing, took me by the hand and led me back to my room. He stood tall, smiled confidently, used a signal for quiet, made his expectations crystal clear and put structure into my lesson. Before long, and to my surprise, these little monsters became, if not angelic, then at least an entirely manageable, ordinary class. Thus, I realised that blaming the kids would never work; in fact, it was simply wrong. Given a clear lead and a structure to work within, these children behaved completely differently. Up to that point, I had been one of those teachers who would launch into a lesson, hoping that no 'behaviour' would happen, and if it did, that I could 'manage' it. I thought the children knew what reasonable behaviour looked like. Now, I realised that I could take nothing for granted; this stuff had to be taught.

'But, hang on,' I hear you say. 'I'm already teaching Key Stage 3 modern languages, GCSE Spanish, three periods of PE and I'm bluffing my way through PSHCE with my form every Friday morning. You want me to teach behaviour as well? You cannot be serious!' Well, yes, I am, because you are doing it already. I am just suggesting that you do it deliberately.

Every time you interact with a young person you are teaching them, whether you like it or not. You do it through the choices you make, the language you use and what you are seen to focus on. I was teaching behaviour when I defended the right of pupils like Nick to feel safe and valued in my classroom. You are teaching behaviour when you stop on the corridor to answer a question, when you intervene to prevent someone running, when you respond to a pupil who wants you to sign their sponsor form for a charity event or when you simply acknowledge them as they pass. All this is teaching behaviour. You are communicating your expectations, your priorities, your values and your grasp of the fact that you are an event in their lives, not the other way around.

Of course, you can go an entirely different way; you might choose to radiate self-pity. Why, oh why must these irritating children ruin my life? Imagine the behaviour that this attitude elicits from children! It is common sense. In *Restorative Practice*, Mark Finnis asks, 'Culture exists in every organisation, but is yours by design or by default?'[1] so it may as well be deliberate, and that means explicitly telling the kids what your values and expectations are and applying them relentlessly. Pupils may live by all manner of codes in their communities – and manners and morals may vary widely in their homes – but the best schools insist that 'this is the way we do things here.'

---

1   Finnis, *Restorative Practice*, p. 29.

Tell them what you want

I was recently in a secondary English class. The teacher, Mr Z, was struggling to maintain quiet. Pupils were chatting, calling out to each other and generally being quite rude. He flitted from one to the other, criticising their behaviour and dishing out various kinds and levels of warning. He was getting nowhere until, to my surprise, he came to the back of the room and asked me for advice. I am not used to this; I generally observe and give advice later, but I thought, 'Fair enough, if I have the cheek to intrude on this guy's lesson, he has every right to expect some practical help.'

'Tell them what you want, and keep telling them,' I whispered. So, he returned to the front of the class and set about it: 'Facing me and listening, please.' I would much rather he had said, 'Listening, thank you,' but this was a good start. He said this simple phrase, and then he began to repeat it, hesitantly at first, but with increasing conviction. For the first time that lesson, and probably for weeks, the class were hearing an explicit description of what Mr Z wanted.

As he continued to repeat this simple instruction, the classroom, which had been a blur, slowly seemed to come into focus. The noise level reduced. Pupils who had been sitting sideways began to face more towards the front. Behaviour was by no means perfect, but Mr Z was able to teach. We tend to take it for granted that classes know what good behaviour is and are wilfully denying it to us. In fact, they are usually waiting to be led.

I watched an IT lesson in Bradford not long ago. The teacher, Mr M, called loudly for attention and then began his lesson. Some of the girls at the back continued their conversation underneath his rather lacklustre description of the task. Some of the boys leant across from their tables to nudge, mock and generally irritate their friends, as only Year 9 boys can.

I left the room after twenty minutes or so and wrote some notes for Mr M, which included these thoughts:

Would you like the class to

- Sit at their PCs with both legs under the desk?
- Speak only in a low 'partner' voice to each other?
- Speak only to pupils on the same table?

■ Turn completely away from the screen and face you when you call for their attention?

If the answer to these is yes, then you need to teach them to do these things. At present you seem willing to put up with less, so they give you less. Think about how you teach anything else: clear instructions, lots of repetition and praise when they get it right, understanding that it is mixed ability and they will learn at varying speeds. It is the same with behaviour. You might be taking it for granted that they know what you want. You seemed a little annoyed that they were not 'well behaved'. You need to tell them explicitly what you want, again and again, until you get it. Think about routines you can teach them in the first five minutes that will teach them these behaviours.

And tell them *succinctly*. You can be more economic with your language when addressing inappropriate behaviour. It will save you time and get faster results – for example, instead of, 'We should be getting on with this in silence, Year 7,' you might try, 'I need silence, Year 7.' Similarly, instead of, 'I shouldn't be hearing any talking,' you might try, 'One voice, thank you.'

On the other hand, there are times when desired behaviour might be described in more detail. You might be in the habit of praising those who are getting it right – something like, 'Thank you, X, thank you, Y.' How about going one step further and letting the whole class know why the pupils being highlighted are praiseworthy? For example, 'Thank you, X, you are giving me active listening, your hands are empty and your eyes are on me.' Now, others know what you are after and they are better placed to follow suit.

What you accept ...

When the National Strategies came to an end, I was out of a job and needed to pay the mortgage, so I set out as a supply teacher. Teaching someone else's lesson to kids you do not know is tough. I did OK, and one of the main reasons I usually won on points was that I set out my stall very clearly right from the start. One particular week brought a very interesting challenge – going back to the school where I had been a head of year several years earlier. I used to have some clout there, but now? Nobody knew me. I was just Johnny Supply-Teacher as far as the pupils were concerned, and as they shuffled into the science lab, they were almost literally rubbing their hands with glee at the prospect of running a supply teacher ragged.

Suddenly, a girl came cartwheeling in, all flailing arms and girly whoops. I pointed to the door and raised my voice a little: 'Thank you!' She knew the game was up and she marched back to the doorway. I calmly intercepted her, made eye contact and smiled. 'Look,' I said. 'Don't worry, we haven't fallen out, but there's a right way and a wrong way to enter the classroom – and that wasn't the right way, was it?' She did not look overjoyed, but she nodded and walked off to her seat. Just then I heard a voice at the back of the room, one lad to another: 'This one's not takin' any shit!'

Well, sir took some, but as the staff in the prep room will tell you, not too much. My expectations had been clear. This is an important principle: what you accept, you establish. If I had allowed that girl to continue unchallenged, I would have given the green light to all sorts of behaviour, as if I had said, 'Hey, that's fine, bawl and scream all you like.' Yet, I still see staff who sit at their laptops while kids ramble in and reel about, and they ignore all this until they decide they want quiet, when the day is already lost. The deliberate, explicit and unwavering strictness I am arguing for is a benign one; not a wish to confront or repress the children but simply an unwavering commitment to 'This is the way we do it here.'

Another example: it was September, and so I had a new GCSE English class. I got to the classroom in plenty of time. When the pupils arrived, I had them line up and indicated that they should fill up from the back in reverse alphabetical order (the contrarian in me at that time liked doing the opposite of what most colleagues did). The middle row started with a girl and next I called for Kai, who I had not previously encountered. He appeared to be the sort of boy who spells the word girl 'gurl', and he stomped in, snorting over his shoulder a loud, snotty 'God!'

I gestured towards the door. 'Kai? Let's try that again, shall we?' Kai responded better than I had hoped, calmly taking his place. He was no trouble after that. Later that lesson I conducted my usual questionnaire. Kai's dad was in the military and often away for long periods. It is not too much of a stretch to imagine that he needed a father figure. The structure and attention had gone down well. We were sorted.

The whole-school dimension

There is, of course, a whole-school dimension to expectations. Many new teachers find that they arrive full of idealistic zeal, only to be swallowed up by the repressive regime that holds sway in the school. Swimming against the tide is hard and you may only be rewarded with the scorn that my friends and I reserved for Mr Schaedel (see Chapter 5).

To put it another way, how your pupils respond to you will to some extent reflect how they feel about the school. In a school where inspirational leadership promotes and embodies simple rules and a clear ethos that all the adults live daily, you will receive far fewer challenges because behaviour is a team sport. When your pupils know that every adult in the school will speak the same language, strike the same deal and stick to it with the same level of relentlessness, when they see that it is not worth trying to play mum off against dad or experimenting with bad behaviours just to see what happens – because they know what will happen – their behaviour will improve. I point this out here just to stress that one individual can only do so much, so be realistic and do not take it personally.

Another limitation is that, as the newcomer, you might find yourself teaching the 'sink' group. It appals me that this still goes on, but it does. Some bright spark has the idea that since many of Year 9 will not be taking the subject in Year 10, let us put all the low-achieving, disaffected pupils in the same group. It is a counsel of despair and recipe for disaster. The kids are not stupid. They know they are the 'unteachables' and so they respond accordingly: 'We're the lowest of the low, so let's show the grown-ups just how low we can go.' Faced with a class like that, the approaches and strategies that I recommend in this book, and the ones I refer to by other leaders in the field, will help you, but the situation will be very hard to turn around. The sink group is the ultimate self-fulfilling prophecy.

Two types of expectations

I am often amused by teachers who tell me that they have 'high expectations'. Sometimes they are wearing leather patches at the elbow, sometimes not. When I ask what these high expectations consist of, they trot out the usual list: good manners, a respectful attitude, hard work, smart uniform, enthusiasm, willingness to follow the rules about equipment and so on. And who could argue against such a list? These behaviours make our job a pleasure when we find them.

But when I then ask the same staff to think about their most challenging class and tell me what behaviour they expect to see, the list looks rather different: shouting out, throwing things, answering back and so on. This demonstrates that the word 'expectations' is fraught with danger. If you expect behaviour to be dreadful next lesson, then, in reality, you have low expectations. And consider this: if your high standards and your realistic assessment of the behaviour you are likely to encounter are not the same, with which set of expectations do you meet the class?

I spoke in Chapter 4 about the vital importance of meet and greet. Sadly, I have seen this done as meet and berate. The teacher stands, arms folded, in the doorway, scowling down the corridor as if sucking a putrefying slug, hoping to put the fear of God into children at long distance. These are the teachers who saw a 'Catch it, Bin it, Kill it' poster displayed during the pandemic and hoped it was the new behaviour policy. They use the meet and greet to make an overt display of their negative expectations: 'You will misbehave today, and I will be angry. This is not going to be fun.' That lesson can only go one way.

How else do staff communicate their expectations?

Pupils will find out what your true expectations are whether you tell them or not. They leak out in a number of ways.

A tidy room is ...

Earlier in this chapter, I described the science cover lesson where I sent a Year 10 girl out to come back in, in order to demonstrate my boundaries. What I did not describe is the teacher's desk, which was buried beneath a mountain of paper so enormous that only the top of my head can have been visible to the class. I would not have been surprised had a lost Japanese soldier emerged from this A4 jungle at any moment, unaware that the Second World War had ended. At the end of the lesson, I staggered into the prep room, having, I considered, come out on top after a fairly trying time.

'What did you do to them?' asked one of the technicians.

'What do you mean?' I replied.

'We thought you'd gagged them!'

'You mean, they're *worse than that* for their normal teacher?!'

'Oh yes!' they chorused, adopting that knowing, wide-eyed nod that people give when sharing particularly salacious bits of gossip, and said no more.

That desk told me everything I needed to know. The paperwork, the pupils, the lesson – they all have to demonstrate genuine high expectations if we are going to survive in a classroom.

As I have said, I visit lessons a lot, coaching new teachers, giving them pointers and suggesting strategies. Before a lesson starts, I can frequently be found bouncing about on the carpet, pouncing on stray bits of paper, plastic and pencil shavings, like a thrush on a lawn stabbing at worms. I do this not only because I am a bit of a Womble at heart, because I want to look helpful and because it shows the teacher that I am not an Ofsted inspector, but also because I need them to know that your gaff needs to look tidy when the class come in. If all about them seems ordered and cared for, there is a chance that your class will follow suit, but if your room resembles a scrapyard after a hurricane blew through, do not be surprised if behaviour is correspondingly ragged.

Display is another important aspect of this. It will show that you expect to focus on learning. My best advice is to treat this like advertising: think through how your display will play in the minds of your classes. What are the most relevant messages? Too many classrooms are festooned with posters advertising long-abandoned initiatives or promoting two or even three out-of-date behaviour policies, lofty statements by great philosophers and statesmen that are never explained, the 'word of the week' from three weeks ago and notices for clubs that ceased running last term. Posters on the wall that say 'Bully-Free Zone' do not have some voodoo power over behaviour. They only contribute if they are referred to regularly and pointed towards in order to challenge inappropriate behaviour.

Punctuality

Another aspect of you that says 'I care' is arriving on time. Break duties, colleagues who want to bash your ear and needy pupils can delay us if we let them, but our primary function is to get in front of that class and teach. If you can get there first, your pupils are safer, you have the opportunity to meet and greet positively, you get to demonstrate that this is your turf and you can organise your resources more easily.

Facial expression

One of the biggest mistakes we can make is to look miserable. On rare occasions there might be a good reason for a long face. If your partner telephones you at work to say that a tree has flattened the house, the insurance company will not pay up and she has arranged for you both to live at her parents' place for the next six months, you might look a tad downcast. But that is a rarity; it is in our interests to look like we want to be there.

Children are drawn towards stable, resilient adults, and if you look like you are stuck in a job you hate, that does not inspire confidence or respect. I have sometimes been moved to say to teachers when sharing feedback on their lessons, 'You look like your mates went down the pub and left you with this class.' If the adult looks like he is lumbered, the children will let him know just how lumbered he can be.

You need to radiate optimism and confidence to show that you expect good things. In Chapter 2, we looked at acting calm. Another part of the act is to make a show of expecting the best possible behaviour. It is preferable if your care and commitment to the children's well-being are genuine, but at the start of your career it is quite OK to act the confidence bit. Look for that confident version of you and play it to the hilt.

Staying in the moment should help you to stay positive. I once worked with a team of lunchtime supervisors on their behaviour management. Very nice ladies, they began the dinner interval with beaming smiles, determined to create a positive atmosphere. Then, once the rush was over and pupils were sitting eating, I saw their smiles disappear as the minutes passed. I watched them as they stood staring into space and began to daydream, and pretty soon, to a woman, you would think they were sucking sour sweets – all furrowed brows, pursed lips and blazing eyes. Eventually, I trained them to catch one another frowning and give a little signal to say 'lighten up'. When I called back a few weeks later, they delightedly told me that the strategies I shared had worked a treat with the little ones and the older ones but, most importantly, with their husbands; no wonder they looked so pleased!

I visited a nurture group recently, at the teacher's request, as her little charges were becoming grumpy and difficult. I was astonished to find that this woman, who had been entrusted with boosting the confidence of the most vulnerable pupils in the school, was managing behaviour with a put-upon look as if her choice had been this or the firing squad. She did not smile once. No wonder their behaviour was poor. These kinds of pupils have usually had a bellyful of disapproval – that is why, in many cases, they are vulnerable in the first place.

Posture

There is a reason that matadors do not slouch. If you stand still, stand tall and appear confident, you will look the part. You are the (warm, empathetic) boss here and everyone must know it before you speak. (For more on posture see 'The physical script' in Chapter 2.)

Voice

Your voice says a lot about your expectations, and the most basic element of your voice is its volume. I was working in a successful comprehensive in northern England once, watching an advanced skills maths teacher, Mr G, with his Year 9 group. Mr G was not aggressive or mean, but he spoke like this: 'GOOD MORNING YEAR 9! TODAY WE'LL BE LOOKING AT CALCULATING THE AREA OF SHAPES, SO TURN TO PAGE 57 OF *I LOVE MATHS* AND OPEN YOUR EXERCISE BOOKS!'

It was deafening. My ears really hurt – and I have seen The Who five times. A girl in the third row stuck her fingers in her ears, turned towards me and mouthed, 'Too loud!' Mr G never even noticed. Had a nearby jet broken the sound barrier or a car backfired in the corridor, we would not have heard it. Even the gardener's strimmer outside the window that regularly destroyed my poetry lessons never reached this level.

Speaking at rock concert volume is inadvisable for so many reasons:

- It is unnatural. People do not speak to one another like that (unless they are in a retirement home and their batteries have faded), so why would you talk to a class in that manner? It makes you seem distinctly odd, and pupils are unlikely to engage with you.

- If you speak this loudly, it is unpleasant for the class and probably exhausting for you. Worst of all, it gives the class the impression that you are not expecting them to listen. It is as if you are anticipating trouble and have decided that WORDS will PIN them to their SEATS. If you lower the volume, you will show that you expect to be listened to.

- It is hard for you to listen when you are making all that noise. Never value your content more than your audience. If you are steadily bellowing at the class, you will be unaware of how you are coming over and assessment for learning will be a pipe dream. After all, this maths teacher seemed completely oblivious to the girl with her fingers in her ears. And if he missed that, what else was he missing?

- It says 'We do not have a relationship. You will not engage with me, so I am going to bludgeon my way into your consciousness.' If there is a recording of Gandhi yelling or the Dalai Lama using a loud hailer, I have yet to hear it.

Another aspect of your voice that you might want to lower is the pitch. It was Mrs Thatcher who famously worked on her voice to remove the tinny upper-class cadences, learning to pronounce 'house' as 'house' and not 'hice'. Her voice actually dropped by 46 Hz.[2]

I would not suggest that you copy the Iron Lady in any other aspects of your professional life, but, for female teachers in particular, there is a danger that your voice, which may be relatively high-pitched to begin with, will soar ever skywards as you raise it in moments of stress. This is another argument for speaking quietly, of course. Some voices can become buzz saws and are really hard to listen to. Once more, the best way is to get yourself recorded and hear it first-hand.

With-it-ness

You absolutely must know what is going on and be seen to know what is going on. If small objects are flying around the room, and you do not notice, the sharks will smell blood. If there is chatter while you talk, and you do nothing, then you have just established that it is OK to talk while sir/miss does. Basically, you want to be a goat or a rabbit – they have pretty much 360-degree vision. You do not want to be an owl with tunnel vision having to turn your head to see stuff.

Think about your positioning too. When pupils need individual attention, do not forget about what is going on behind your back. This may seem basic, but you would be surprised how many times I have to call teachers out on it, which perhaps points to the underlying issue. You have got to *want* to know about everything that is going on, based on the belief that you are in charge as this is your gaff, your rules, and you can and will take decisive action when you see or hear something that contravenes your clearly established expectations.

---

2   See https://www.youtube.com/watch?v=28_0gXLKLbk.

Communicating expectations

I was watching a PGCE student, we will call him Mr S, just the other day. Year 7 science in a very challenging inner-city school in the North of England. The pupils arrived in a boisterous mood, dragging their chairs about and banging them down in their places. There were coloured A4 pictures of various terrains on the desks. Instructions on the board said they should match up these pictures with their descriptions, which were also on the tables. The teacher had clearly decided to avoid struggling to gain pupils' attention at the start of the lesson; instead, he had set up this activity to act like flypaper, and once all the flies were stuck fast he would attempt the register. By the time he got around to calling the register, ten minutes of messy, unfocused and silly behaviour had passed.

Mistake number one. As we saw in Chapter 4, pupils need a whole-class welcome. They need the adult to establish a moment of quiet and focus at the very start of the lesson. Even on supply, I would always begin with, 'Let's have a bright and breezy "Yes, sir" or "Yes, Mr Baker" in answer to your name.' Taking the register was my chance to set the tone, to treat pupils with respect and to demand it from them – and, quite honestly, there is something about the reply 'Here' that is just dreary and life-sapping.

Anyway, the lesson deteriorated quite rapidly. Mr S nagged the class constantly about shouting out and several times raised his voice to complain about their behaviour. Then, about half an hour in, he started putting names on the board. Some of these named pupils continued messing about and Mr S adorned their names with a tick.

The class continued to fall out, wander about and ignore the task, so Mr S summoned on-call. Ten minutes later, a fierce woman in a trouser suit entered the room and gave the whole class a proper roasting. All pupils whose names were on the board were to report to her at lunchtime on pain of death, or thereabouts.

Every behaviour that you do not want to see must be challenged, not by the parent shouting at it or by the child whinging about it, but challenged by the adult, stating fact about whole-school expectations and the inevitable consequences of ignoring them. The key message at this point is to implement your system from the start of the lesson.

A word on implementing a system. I am frequently told by staff who have sent half the class to on-call that 'I was using the behaviour policy.' It is odd how selective staff can be. The behaviour policy in question usually says something about taking a positive approach, showing respect to pupils, using the least intrusive techniques, de-escalating, having a quiet word and so on. Yet, some staff appear to treat this in the same way that I treat the financial pages in the Sunday paper. They flick past them to get to the bit they are interested in – the series of sanctions. Challenging all behaviours that do not meet your expectations is not the same as using them as steps on a ladder towards removal.

Some teachers do not display these regular overreactions; they save it up for one big blow-out instead. The 'sod-it moment' comes when a teacher has put up with minor indiscretions for maybe fifteen or twenty minutes, speaking over the shouting out and managing with pleas and threats. Eventually they have had enough, think, sod it – that's it, and bellow at the class or at some poor unfortunate individual. It leads to accusations of unfairness (what about the other twenty people who shouted out?) and it poisons the atmosphere. Such moments can be avoided if the rules apply from the very start, which they always should.

It is hard to express just how vital positive expectations are; in essence, we see what we look for. There are, of course, schools where the challenges come thick and fast, but even here, with the most trying classes, giving the impression that today is a new day and you are optimistic about today's lesson is crucial. Every successful teacher follows this recipe: leave the pupils in no doubt about exactly what you want and give them the impression that you confidently expect to get it. You may not get it there and then, but over time and with persistence you can succeed.

Takeaways

- We need to tell our pupils explicitly what behaviours we want to see.

- The same children behave very differently for teachers who do and do not make their expectations clear.

- You are an event in the child's life, not the other way around.

- Be aware of the many ways in which you communicate your expectations without meaning to.

- Your expectations are what you genuinely expect to see; anything else is just a wish list.

NOW TRY THIS:

Take a blank piece of A4 paper and hold it in front of you in a portrait orientation. Fold it vertically down the middle, creating two columns.

In the left-hand column, list pupil behaviours that harm learning.

In the right-hand column, against each of the items on the left, list the exact positive opposite. (Adding 'not' as in 'Not talking out of turn' will not do; you need to list the positive alternative to each inappropriate behaviour.)

Now tear the paper along the crease and throw the left-hand column away.

You are now looking at your behaviour curriculum. When do you teach each of these things? How do you acknowledge them when they occur? Do you model them yourself?

Chapter 7

MODELLING

In the previous chapter, we saw how we must teach behaviour deliberately or risk doing it badly by default. We looked at how staff communicate their expectations and how this has a massive effect on the way in which young people behave.

In this chapter, the focus is on how we lead pupil behaviour through our own example, or 'modelling' as it is known. I have emphasised elsewhere in this book how the best schools proclaim, 'This is the way we do it here', and now we will explore how the best teachers incorporate this within a strong sense of 'This is how we do it *in my classroom*.'

Mrs Baines teaches me a lesson

The best CPD I ever received was delivered directly to me by a parent at parents' evening, one dark November night. I had just been served a cup of tea by a Year 11 pupil who had clearly never made a cup of tea in his life, but I was grateful nonetheless. Mrs Baines was a rosy-cheeked woman, quite old-fashioned in her hat and coat, with prominent teeth. She sat down, gave a quiet 'Michael Baines' and listened intently as I trotted out all the usual chat about her son's grades, what the class had been studying, what we would be moving on to soon and all the rest of it. She thanked me and made to go, but I called her back:

'Before you go, Mrs Baines, there's just one more thing …'

'Oh?' she replied, settling back down in her chair.

I leant forward so I could keep my voice down: 'It's just that Michael can be … how do I put this? … a little *giddy* sometimes …'

Mrs Baines looked thoughtful. 'Well, that is interesting, Mr Baker. You say Michael is giddy. I've just been talking with Mr Varley (Mr Varley was a

111

well-established, mild-mannered teacher with twenty-five years of experience) and Mr Varley says that Michael is quite calm in class.' It was Mrs Baines' turn to lean forward: 'But then … Mr Varley's quite calm, isn't he?'

This devastating verdict on *my* classroom behaviour was delivered with absolutely no malice; in fact, Mrs Baines could not have been nicer about it. I thanked her for coming and, yes, you have guessed it, another penny dropped. My God, it is not Michael who needs to change, it is *me*! I thought about my joke-making, my clowning around and teasing of pupils, my tendency to stir up the class and then get annoyed when they could not calm down at the drop of a hat – and it all began to make sense. As parents' evening petered out, I was left alone with just that cup of tea and my own thoughts for company, both equally appalling. A terrible truth had dawned: everything I wanted my pupils to be, I had to be first.

Some years later, visiting a Wakefield school, I met an elderly, sour-faced teacher of woodwork. He might have learned his trade working on the ark for Noah, that is how old he was. Now, please do not get me wrong, when I come across teachers in their fifties and sixties who are as enthused about the job and as committed to the learning and well-being of children as they were when they first started out, there is nothing I find more moving and worthy of the very highest praise. But when people hang on, long after their passion for the job and interest in young people has faded, well, that is not doing anyone any favours.

Anyway, he fixed me with a watery-eyed stare from behind a pair of old-fashioned, thick-framed spectacles, and in his equally thick Yorkshire accent, at a speed more usually associated with tortoises and garden snails, he eventually let fly, 'They … show… *ab-so-lute-*ly … *no* … en-*thooooo*-siasm … *what*-so … *ever!*' And why that might be? I wondered.

Wearing the crown

Children are people. But that does not mean the classroom is a democracy, unless you teach at Summerhill.[1] The class is a pack and you are its leader. Becoming that classroom leader is a little like a coronation. You must get

---

1   At Summerhill School in Suffolk, which was founded in 1921 by A. S. Neill, lessons are optional and pupils are free to choose how and what to learn, so long as their actions do not harm others.

used to wearing the crown and sitting on the throne, not because you are on a power trip but because you need to look as if you are comfortable as top dog in the room. (I know dogs do not wear crowns, outside of Crufts, but you see what I mean.) Most of us possess a bunch of insecurities, learned in childhood, that we drag around like a noisy ball and chain, and assuming you do not have bolt cutters, you will need to at least gather up that ball and chain and place it where your subjects cannot see it.

If, as a child, you put salt instead of sugar in your little sister's tea or stole a milk bottle from your elderly neighbour's doorstep, your pupils will not know this, and you can keep your shame and regret firmly out of sight. You are an authority figure now, like it or not. A kind and empathetic one, naturally, but an authority figure nonetheless. Your classes will expect you to boss the room (nicely) and lead the pack, so if you fidget, start every sentence with, 'Can we just …?' or lavish everyone and everything with unmerited gushing praise, they will quite likely decide that you are not to be listened to or respected. They will go back to arranging their social lives or hairdos, while you stand fuming.

You can practise entering the room, practise welcoming the class, practise your posture, your gestures and your tone of voice, practise the scripts that we looked at in Chapter 2 and practise this whole performance until it feels perfectly natural. When you look and sound like you believe you deserve respect, you are halfway to getting it.

Acting your authentic self

Finding your teacher persona can be a challenge. If you are unnatural, the children will not relate to you, and if you are too unguardedly yourself, you might say and do stuff you regret. There is a happy medium to be found. Your teacher persona has to be a revelation of your authentic self *and* it also has to be an act. In other words, you have to employ a version of your authentic self.

For example, most of you would be mad to try to be the hard man/woman because it is not in your nature and the children will see through you in seconds. But you probably have a slightly firmer side that you call on when you need to assert yourself with relatives, shopkeepers or nuisance phone calls. You might begin by borrowing (carefully) from that version of yourself.

Build a persona from all these selves that seems confident and in charge. When I deliver training, teachers sometimes believe that the confident fellow they see parading about in front of them and getting big laughs (on a good day) is entirely me. But it is just one version of me. There are other versions available, and not all of them are so appealing to listen to; just ask my partner or my children.

It's a tough world out there

Children are subject to all manner of influences. My dad, who was born in 1935, remembers his head teacher addressing the entire school in assembly one morning and warning them about a popular singer whose irresponsible, dissolute behaviour was setting a very bad example. 'I don't want to hear his name mentioned in my school,' he told them. Who was this icon of depravity, this bestial fiend, presenting an imminent threat to the fabric of Western civilisation? Bing Crosby. I wonder what the head teacher would have made of Marilyn Manson?

In 2022, the children we teach are beset with all manner of influences. Social networking has given them fake friends, sexting and around-the-clock bullying. When I was being picked on in the 1970s, I could get on the bus and leave the bullies behind; not any more. And popular culture? Just look at it. The weakest in society are herded in front of cameras, stunned by stage lights and prodded into slaughtering each other, until the host hoses the blood off the tiles. Celebrities flaunt their Photoshopped bodies, airbrushed faces and fantasy lifestyles, selling self-loathing to the rest of us.

Meanwhile, on the streets where our children live, there are gangs who offer belonging, commitment and pride but deliver drugs, violence and imprisonment. And, as The Clash once sang, 'What do we have for entertainment?' The answer is soaps full of drunken, selfish whiners emoting about their base motivations. And this is taking place in a world where, if climate change does not get us, a random asteroid, nuclear war or global pandemic will. In the face of all this, it never ceases to amaze me how lovely and how moral the vast majority of young people are. It shows that, despite what we sometimes think, most parents do a very good job of raising their children, who care about those around them and want to make the world a better place. 95% of the children in our schools are a pleasure to teach. Nevertheless, when they are in school, our pupils need a deliberate, principled lead from us, especially the ones who lack that stable parental guidance and support.

Getting it wrong: teachers behaving badly

If we fail to live by the code we promote with children, they will see through us. They will know that we are not sincere and that our protested beliefs and values are nothing but a front for our need to control. So, pop pickers, here is my countdown of this week's top ten adult behaviour fails:

10. Interrupting a colleague's lesson without knocking or apologising.

9. Lecturing those present about the absence of those who are not.

8. Taking the register on the sly during prayers in assembly.

7. Introducing today's lesson as if informing a patient that the prognosis is not good.

6. Performing the meet and greet in a style better suited to the custody suite in your local police station.

5. Patrolling the corridor with a mournful, end-of-the-world-is-nigh expression.

4. Making jokes at pupils' expense but being unable to take a joke.

3. Refusing to listen to children.

2. Sarcasm.

1. Having favourites.

Getting it right

The government once supported the teaching of social and emotional aspects of learning in schools. It became known as SEAL and was a massive hit in primary schools where it has left a solid legacy. It was less successful in secondary, and explaining that is another book entirely. When reflecting on the behaviours we need to model for children in schools, I can think of no better framework than the five domains of SEAL: self-awareness, managing feelings, empathy, motivation and social skills.

1. Self-awareness

Some of our pupils are crippled by self-consciousness but self-awareness is quite different. Knowing your strengths, and the areas in which you are still a work in progress, breeds confidence and also humility.

Apologising is a good example of self-awareness in action. When you realise that a joke you made was inappropriate or that you have overreacted to some minor infringement, a simple apology models for pupils the behaviour that you would like to see from them when they have gone too far. After all, how can they make a sincere apology if they have never seen one?

I was at a rehearsal for our school play back in 1977. The production that year was *War and Peace*. Yes, I know. Anyway, I was one of several boys standing around the piano with the director, the late and much missed Mr Vine, before rehearsal began one afternoon, and someone complained about fitting in rehearsals around his homework. I spoke up saying, 'We've *all* got *homework* to do!' Mr Vine scowled. He pointed his finger at me and thundered, 'Get out then, go home!' He had completely misunderstood. 'But …' I tried to protest, but it was no good. 'Go home!' he bellowed.

I was crushed. I had no option but to shove my script into my satchel and creep off home. I believe that Clive Brill, an older boy (who went on to become a producer for the BBC), turned to Mr Vine and gently explained that I had been trying to support him.

Next morning, I had just entered the building when Mr Vine found me on the stairs and, fair play to him, he could not apologise enough. He must have been patrolling the corridors since the school doors had opened, hoping to find me, and his sincere apology went a long a way to mending my feelings. In a school where brutality and sarcasm were the norm, it was almost worth suffering the bollocking just to have a teacher treat me with such extravagant decency.

Using yourself as a model learner is another way to model self-awareness; being prepared to admit you do not know something and are willing to learn from your pupils. In Ken Loach's classic film *Kes* (and, of course, in Barry Hines' novel), Mr Farthing goes out of his way to enter young Billy's world and learn from him about the care of a kestrel. This willingness to learn from a pupil is also an example of the shared vulnerability that I referred to in Chapter 5.

Accepting the responsibility of being the boss in the room, and acting accordingly, is an act of self-awareness. You demand respect because you know that you deserve it and because you give it, unconditionally. After all, we want our pupils to respect themselves and others, so we must show them what that respect looks like. You may have heard the phrase 'unconditional positive regard', which does not mean that we applaud our pupils when they behave poorly, but it does mean that we make every effort to catch them being good. And when things go wrong, we remain dispassionate, level-headed and respectful, applying consequences when necessary, not in anger or with sardonic relish, but calmly and steadily as the inevitable and well-established result of bad choices made. Plus, by now you will be familiar with my refrain that consequences alone do not teach behaviour and that relationships are far more important.

2. Managing feelings

The other day I was in an assistant principal's office when a sweet little girl appeared at the door. She was about 10 years old but small for her age, with panda-sized bags beneath each eye.

Miss S: Yes, Kerry-Jo?

Kerry-Jo: Miss, have you seen that red plastic flower, what was in the learning support unit?

Miss S: Yes, Kerry-Jo, I saw Jason with it at morning break.

Kerry-Jo (detonating): I'll fuckin' *kill* the little wanker!

I can only imagine what kind of example Kerry-Jo's parents set her. She was lucky to have staff around her who patiently pointed her towards a better path and steadfastly trod it themselves.

As an adult, your life experience should have provided you with more self-control than Kerry-Jo, and when you show restraint, it will pay you back in spades. Suppose Zak yells at Shaz for taking his pencil case. How will you address this? Now, imagine that five minutes earlier, when Zak dropped his pencil case, you yelled at him? What will you do now? You do not have a leg to stand on. The cliché is spot on: actions speak louder than words.

On the other hand, it often pays to be explicit, so to the pupil who has thumped a smaller child you might say, 'I am very angry about what you have done. I will be back to speak to you when I am calmer.' This demonstrates that you are angry – and, crucially, you are not apologising for being angry – but it also demonstrates that an angry state is not one in which to do important stuff. Angry people should take time and think before they act. When Danny leans too far back on his chair, a deafening crash results and a key moment in your lesson is ruined, the fact that you keep your rattle in your pram will help your pupils to learn that anarchy is best met with order rather than chaos.

Remember my biology teacher? 'Ah, Baker – what snivelling excuse have you got for me this week?' I am all for smiting the wicked but royally humiliating children? He could have said, 'Ah, Baker (we were all addressed by our surnames in this medieval setting) – I'm busy now, but if this is about the homework, we'll speak at the end of the lesson.' This would have set up the probability of a break-time detention with minimal fuss, and it would have shown a great deal more respect.

I have given aspects of behaviour leadership their own chapters for the sake of the structure of the book, but they are, of course, inseparable. For example, establishing routines and planning for behaviour will help you to manage your feelings. In my experience, teachers who lose it do so because they do not know where to go next, and this is often unnecessary. You can predict most of the challenges you will face before the lesson begins. You know that Troy will want to turn around and chat with Eddie, you know that

Liv will shout out and that Callum will have his head on the desk. Think these things through and decide your response ahead of time because planning for behaviour can prevent you being tipped over the edge by it.

Another circumstance that causes the teacher tantrum is getting to the end of your tether. This is no laughing matter. Teaching should be a team sport, but in some schools staff are not supported as they should be, and the ethos-by-default is 'paddle your own canoe'. In circumstances like this, it is no wonder that teachers can feel isolated and even desperate. Even in well-run schools the pressure can get too much, especially if there are challenges in your personal life compounding the professional ones. Self-awareness is vital along with communication. What are the warning signs that you might be on the edge? If you feel like that, talk to a trusted colleague and, if necessary, your line manager.

During my teaching career, if I began to lose my temper it usually meant that I was about to get ill. The precursor to a heavy cold was often an unusual level of irritability. If you know you are not feeling great, factor this into your planning and delivery. A lesson that requires long periods of absolute quiet may not be the best choice in these circumstances. This flexibility comes with experience, so the sooner you can develop it, the better.

Of course, some staff just do react very badly to trivial provocations, but stable, resilient adults should not lose their mind when someone sneezes. I have lost count of the number of pastoral staff who have described being called out to remove a pupil because they dropped a pen, farted or had their coat on. Nine times out of ten it is because the teacher entered the room fearing the pupil concerned and then panicked at the first sign of trouble.

3. Empathy

My physics teacher in Year 9 was the balding Geordie Mr Welsh. He wore a white suit, but this did not signify any special moral qualities. Far from it. He had a habit of grabbing your hair and banging your head on the desk (no, I am not making this up), and he brazenly added 10% to our exam results ('Baker, 28% – we'll make that 38%') purely to save his job.

Anyway, one day I admitted to Mr Welsh that I did not know how to wire a plug. He seemed surprised, so I asked him, nicely, if he would show me how. He reacted as if I had asked him to read me a story and tuck me in. 'No! You're ignorant, lad!' was all he said, and when I repeated my request he repeated the answer. I was ignorant. That was all he had to say. Where was his empathy? I struggle to get inside the head of a teacher who refuses a genuine request like this one. Here was an opportunity to teach some physics, for real, but no.

Empathy means we remember being children; we know what it is like to sit in a classroom or jog around a field. We show empathy when we subtly adjust our lesson plans on a sweltering July afternoon. Empathy helps us to manage our feelings too. It is because we remember being 13 years old that we can refrain from volcanic displays of anger at stupid teenage behaviour.

Empathy drives the efforts of staff to meet and greet with a smile at the gate and in the school foyer. Or it should do. Too often, though, empathy has worn away, leaving only po-faced commands to do with ties, jumpers, shoes and the like. Turning up at school really should not feel like crossing a Stasi checkpoint. Airport security staff would be horrified if they were to witness the sullen, authoritarian manner with which some staff carry out this morning ritual. If a welcome is a welcome, let it be just that.

We also show empathy when we plan our lessons. I described in Chapter 2 the lethal effect that two words can have on a group of adults in training. If I want to provoke instant abject fear, all I need to do is say 'role play'. Grown women tremble. Men find urgent reasons to leave the room. No one likes the idea of public humiliation, which is the underlying worry, I guess. Fair enough, but as I have taken to pointing out, these teachers' pupils will have similar anxieties linked to algebra, Shakespeare and swimming.

Just one caveat about empathy: we must be honest with ourselves. If you are tempted to let Johnny wear his headphones, is this really because you empathise with him or because you cannot face the confrontation?

4. Motivation

Getting the books marked and returned quickly is one way to show you are motivated. In recent years, enlightened senior leadership teams have told staff not to mark *everything*. My daughter's mathematics teacher told me at a parents' evening that he needed to set homework each week so he knew if pupils had understood the work. Assessment for learning had passed him by. I was too polite (and too cowardly) to point this out. Although smart teachers are selective about which pieces of work get a full-on marking, and the workload they face is such that I almost shrink from saying it, getting the work returned in a timely fashion is huge for children. It is a key indicator of your level of commitment to them. And, of course, it is a clear way to model meeting deadlines: 'I want it in by X; you'll get it back by Y.'

Arriving on time for lessons is another way to model motivation: 80% of success, they say, is showing up, and showing up *on time*. I remember a PE teacher who used to arrive late after break on freezing winter mornings to unlock the changing rooms with a steaming mug of coffee in his hand, his cackle audible over our shivers, and then he would demand that we flog ourselves to death on the sports field. I do not think the hypocrisy of it ever dawned. Being on time is the most basic way to show that you are bothered. When the deputy head has to patrol the staffroom at the end of break and prise staff out of their seats, you know the school has a problem.

When I became a head of year, the first thing I was told was, 'You'll be late to all your lessons.' I was doubtful, but as a teaching head of year who had to cram my pastoral role into breaks, lunchtimes and two extra free periods (sorry, *non-contact* periods; free is really not the word), I soon realised. I had to fight hard to prioritise getting to class on time, and thus being on the front foot, ready, calm and organised.

Of course, staying beyond the bell is another way to model motivation. When the teaching day is over, your willingness to stay back and help those who need the homework explaining one more time is massive.

Modelling excitement about today's lesson is vital. If it does not excite you, it will not excite them. What will this hour in your company do for your pupils? What will they be learning that is new and different? What skills will they acquire or sharpen? If you can excite curiosity in children, they will want to learn and all talk of behaviour becomes irrelevant.

When you tackle inappropriate behaviour rather than ignoring it, you are displaying motivation. Nothing dismays pupils more than the teacher who apparently cannot be bothered to protect learning from disruption.

Telling pupils about formal or informal study that you are doing, such as books you are reading or relevant factual TV series you are following, is a marvellous way to show that you are a learner too, and so learning is not merely a painful experience that you are inflicting on the young but a life-long source of joy and inspiration.

5. Social skills

OK, hands up those of you who have done this. You are leading a class discussion and a pupil makes a good point which reminds you of something you want to say to the group, but by the time this registers, you have already invited another pupil to speak. As she is speaking, your mind clings on to the thing you want to say when she is finished. But she does not finish; she carries on, developing her point. Your eyes have glazed over. You are simply waiting for her to pause so you can pounce. You are not listening!

You might also have complained that a pupil's shirt is hanging out before having the good manners to say 'Good morning.' What would it cost – a moment's courtesy before the finger-pointing begins? I was shadowing an assistant head of year the other day. We came across a lone girl on the corridor wearing a bronze puffer jacket. He barely glanced at her and said 'Coat off!' before moving on. Given the workload he had faced that morning, it was understandable, but if we let ourselves get reduced to that level of clapped-out vigilance, we may as well be replaced by artificial intelligence. A central computer linked to CCTV and loudspeakers could easily provide a cry of 'Coat off!' whenever the crime is digitally detected. If these interactions do not require the recognition that the miscreant is a unique person with feelings and intentions, then why dedicate a person to conduct them?

Bill Rogers, being an Australian, would of course begin with 'G'day!' Here in Britain, a 'Morning, gents!' would probably suffice. It takes two seconds to transform the interaction. Before you approach, the child's amygdala is cocked and loaded, ready to classify you as a threat. Why go along with it? A simple 'Afternoon, ladies' is so much more pleasant and effective.

I frequently see teachers fail to welcome the teaching assistant when they enter the room. The teacher begins their lesson and five minutes into it a teaching assistant arrives. Does the teacher pause to say with a smile, 'Good afternoon, Miss Sparrow! Really glad you're joining us – it's the Ancient Romans today. I'll speak to you in a moment'? No, sir does not even look up, he just ploughs on, while the teaching assistant scurries to a seat with her head down, looking about as welcome as a fart in a spacesuit. These are golden opportunities to model social skills between two adults, and they are too frequently missed. A proper welcome would also be a strong signal to the class that these adults are allies who work as a team, and they will support one another should any behaviour difficulties arise.

Teachers are busy people. So much is thrown at them – so many hoops to jump through, boxes to tick and deadlines to meet – that it is all too easy to forget that pupils are watching and following your example. I have been told in recent years, 'Always imagine that the child's parent is sitting on your shoulder and watching how you behave towards their child.' I wish I had been given that advice when I started out.

Takeaways

- Your example is more powerful than your words.

- The social and emotional skills you display are at least as important as your subject content.

- There is a contradiction at the heart of working with young people: you must be authentic and yet you must put on an act.

- If you are not excited about today's lesson, why should your pupils be?

NOW TRY THIS:

Turn to Appendix 3 and note down in the space provided when your pupils see you model the personal qualities listed during the week.

Chapter 8

PRAISE, REWARDS AND OTHER CONSEQUENCES

The positive stuff

Let's start by looking at praise and other rewards. On social media the other day, some wag suggested that perhaps we have been wrong all along and praising pupils is not such a great idea. It was possibly just someone being provocative, hoping to attract Twitter traffic, but there is a grain of truth in there. It depends on what you mean by praise, but to evaluate praise effectively we need to see it from the child's point of view.

Keep it real

I was watching a deputy head teach bottom-set Year 9 maths some years ago, in a tough school in the North of England. I cannot honestly remember what the subject was, but I do remember that he seemed to be channelling the late Jim Bowen, host of *Bullseye*. He stood, legs apart, knees slightly bent, with his arms stuck out and his thumbs up, spouting 'Great! Smashing! Super!' over and over again throughout the entire lesson.

Behaviour was more or less acceptable, but it was not 'great', 'smashing' or even 'super' by any stretch of the imagination. Watching him stand there, spraying positivity like confetti, he reminded me of a firefighter. The 'praise hose' was soaking the room, but I do not believe that any of those pupils got wet. Doubtless, they each imagined his random, directionless praise was meant for someone else.

Be specific

Nowadays, I see well-intentioned staff who go one better. They name the children: 'Thank you, Jane.' 'Thank you, Parvez.' 'Thank you, Kyle.' Yet they fail to explain why these children are praiseworthy.

In recent years, teachers have learned to demystify success in learning, providing model answers, studying mark schemes and outlining success criteria, yet behaviour success criteria remain hidden. We can use praise to make this plain: 'Well done, Eric. Excellent active listening from you. Your eyes are on me and your pen is down. Keep it up!'

I am a lousy golfer because, on those rare occasions when the ball flies off in a satisfying arc towards the green, I have no idea how I managed it. Targeted specific praise can make your learners consciously competent. They will know why the kid on the table next to them was praised, and they will have the opportunity to do the same.

Calibrate it

I frequently meet young teachers who wheel out the big guns, no matter what the situation. Everything is 'Amazing!' or 'Fantastic!' While I salute the energy and enthusiasm of these staff, I need to ask, is it amazing when Dylan takes a seat? Er, no. Is it fantastic when the class get out their planners? Um, nope. When pupils meet our basic expectations that is 'good', 'pleasing' and 'well done'. Praise does not always need to be ten out of ten, and behaviour need not be described in hyperbolic terms.

Pupils are not daft. They know when they have done something extraordinary and they know when they have not. If you go wild for minimum standards, that is all you will get. If someone told me, 'Steve, that's amazing. Walking *and* chewing gum at the same time, brilliant!', it would not motivate me to try harder. I would think they were taking the mickey, or perhaps a bit thick.

I recently watched *The Apprentice* on TV. The candidates had failed to convince a shopkeeper to buy their product. As they left the shop, one of them said, 'Thank you for your time', which is only polite, but the other one said, 'Fantastic!' I had to watch the sequence again to be sure I had heard him right. How can it be fantastic to leave empty-handed?

This bizarre behaviour is symptomatic of an empty-headed, talk-everything-up approach. We need to acknowledge pupils who meet minimum standards and look to praise those who exceed them, but we should not be spraying positive words around willy-nilly. It breeds cynicism and works against genuine connection. Most importantly, there is no need. There is always someone in your class getting it right who would benefit from specific personal praise.

Highlight good behaviour

In any classroom, even in the nightmare scenario, look for those who are getting it right. Give them your attention and acknowledge their behaviour. You may have noticed that if you criticise one child for shouting out, or humming, or tapping a pen, pretty soon a dozen will be doing it. Your attention is fuel for whatever fire is burning. If you hear a lone hum and say, 'Stop the humming!' it will spread like bad news. Ever seen Laurel and Hardy? A teacher who talks constantly about the bad behaviour is like Stan Laurel with his fingers on fire, haplessly setting alight the curtains, the sofa, Oliver Hardy and everything else he touches in his fearful wake.

I was told by a teenage pupil once that 'the only way to get noticed around here is to be a badass.' Who do you notice? Try keeping a tally chart on your desk recording how many times you mention each pupil's name; just thirty minutes' worth will do. Many teachers doing this will find that it is the pupil who will not stay in their seat or constantly chats to a friend who is name-checked most frequently.

Once or twice, I have visited a primary school and found that, no sooner do I get through the front door, than I meet a child, let us call him Edwin, who is frequently in bother and whom everybody loves (and, yes, there is nothing wrong with that), but this Edwin has become some kind of rock star or school mascot, wandering the corridors doing errands for teachers. He is never in class for more than a few minutes, but he is instantly familiar to any visitor. Meanwhile, the children who get it right day after day are the silent, anonymous majority. I am all for loving every child, but we must be careful with the messages we give out.

In your classroom, show the class how to get your attention by giving it where you intend it to go. If you want more good behaviour, the first thing to do is to notice it, and when you have seen it, acknowledge it: 'Jason is on task', 'Sheryl is ready to learn' and so on.

When you are tempted to criticise the poor behaviour of the few, pick out one of the many and highlight their behaviour instead: '*This* young lady is on task, thank you.' '*This* young man is in his chair and has his book out ready.' By doing so, you are reminding the class of your expectations, you are rewarding those who want to side with you, but need encouragement to do so, and you are keeping an optimistic commentary going. The message should be 'Look what is going right', not 'Look what is going wrong.'

Peer praise

You can create opportunities for pupils to praise one another. This might be feedback on each other's work during peer assessment. It could be 'thank yous' on a Friday where pupils thank someone who has been a friend to them earlier in the week. You might need to scaffold this for them with some sentence starters:

- 'I am really grateful to …'

- 'I especially like …'

- 'I like the way that …'

If you have a difficult primary class or secondary form group, one of the best ways to address their behaviour is to play the following game. Send a volunteer out of the room. Ask every pupil to tell you something they like about that pupil. When they return, you read out what has been said and they have to guess who said it. You will soon find that every child wants a turn at being praised.

Rewards

It is important to be giving out more praise than criticism. Your persistent highlighting of the positive behaviours you want to see, even when they might be easily overlooked in the melee, is vital. There is no substitute for showing that you have noticed your pupils, that you are bothered and that you appreciate their efforts. However, some schools and some teachers devote too much time to formal systems of recognition when, in fact, it is the informal, done-in-passing stuff that does the heavy lifting. Rewards are a waste of time if they do not take place within the context of a rewarding relationship.

Take the technology teacher whose lesson I once visited. The routine in this school was that stamps should be awarded in every lesson. The clock had ticked around to within one minute of the hour when someone gently reminded him that everybody's planner needed stamping. With a pained expression and cow-in-the-slaughterhouse body language he said, 'Oh God, I've just remembered your flaming stamps. Righto! (heavy sigh) Line up at my desk. Open your planners ... Come on, we haven't got all day!' The class lined up with their planners out, looking terrified. Each book was slipped under his nose and stamped with impatient aggression: flip-BANG ... flip-BANG ... flip-BANG ... The bell went, the chairs were going up and it was chaos, punctuated only by flip-BANG and a running commentary along the lines of, 'I don't know why I bother ...' It would be hard to imagine a less rewarding activity.

It takes an act of imaginative empathy to see how your reward will be received. As I never tire of saying, there is no substitute for knowing your pupils. Some love to be publicly acknowledged, and some would rather die. I once led a course for head teachers, over three days set a month apart. After the first of these, a head teacher went back to her Lincolnshire school with a renewed conviction that 'we need to be positive with Lewis.' I know this because she told me at the second session a month later. Anyway, she found a young teaching assistant to work with Lewis, who set about, as instructed, 'being positive' with the youngster. She took to bouncing in each morning declaring, 'Hallo Lewis – how are you?' in a dementedly jolly voice, with a birthday-party-clown-on-cocaine energy level. Lewis marched off, burst into the head's office, pointed behind him in the direction of the teaching assistant and demanded, 'Why's she taking the piss?'

Positive is as positive feels. If the child does not feel positive after your interaction, then you have not been positive. You will know the feeling from when you ask for a hug from your partner and they try saying encouraging things instead. It just annoys you, when all you wanted was the hug. Positive is not in the giving, it is in the receiving.

A word about whole-class rewards. The class must believe that the reward is deserved. Many times, I have seen the teacher who says, 'Look, if you are good today, we can play a game on the whiteboard in the last ten minutes of the lesson.' Behaviour goes on to be appalling and the teacher repeatedly threatens the class with, 'There will be no game on the whiteboard today unless things improve', but the class keep pleading and cajoling until, under tremendous pressure, the teacher wilts and the noisy, uncooperative class gets its reward anyway.

Your class must know that if they receive a treat, they have earned it; and if they do not cooperate, the treat will not happen. I know that sounds blindingly obvious, but I have seen the opposite happen too many times not to mention it.

So, please make every effort to notice and acknowledge your pupils' cooperation and hard work. And remember that, especially for those who struggle to behave, a thumbs-up and a 'well done' from someone they trust, right now, is far more powerful than a raffle ticket for a mountain bike that won't be drawn until next term.

The negative stuff

It is sometimes necessary to inflict unwanted consequences, which can feel negative for you and the child, but this must be framed within a developing relationship. The pupils who cause you the most grief are very often seeking a connection with you, and finding where your boundaries lay is part of that. The consequences you enact for behaviour are a key marker of your approach. They will show the child whether you are bothered, whether you simply want revenge or whether you are looking to help them become their best self.

The pyramid of pain

Some schools install rigid systems designed to deter poor behaviour by making sure potential miscreants are crystal clear about the consequences they face. As if deterrence worked! The pyramid of punishment progresses from C1 (consequence 1) through to C2, C3, C4 and beyond.

I have seen it many times. Mr Smythe is talking to his Year 8 class about the Romans. Jake shows no interest in Julius Caesar and turns to chat to his mate in the row behind.

Mr Smythe: Coins bearing Julius Caesar's image – Jake, that's your C1 – have been found as far apart as …

Jake (*jumping to his feet*): What the hell?

Now, maybe Jake really was the only one talking, and maybe he is a nice boy from a nice home who has learned to self-regulate and can reason with himself that this minor punishment is not the end of the world, and, after all, he was a little slow to notice that Mr Smythe had called for quiet. Or maybe Jake spent last night witnessing domestic violence for the umpteenth time, and so he is just a little bit sensitive to unjust displays of naked power, and perhaps he noticed that several other people were also talking but sir was focused on Jake because he is 'trouble'. So, Jake answers back and sir gives him a C2. Jake takes strong exception to this and we are off. He ends up storming out with the words 'C4!' ringing in his ears.

Pupils like Jake have been let down all their lives by adults who refused to engage with them. They have not formed secure attachments with loving adults and so they do not regulate their behaviour well. An adult dishing out consequences and refusing to engage is the very last thing they need, so their only way to escape this hellish situation is to escalate their behaviour in order to get sent out.

Incredibly, some staff use this process in ways that its designer did not foresee, standing over the child with an accusatory finger, pointing at their coat: 'Get the coat off. No? C1 … I said get it off. No? C2 then … Third time of asking? Right, C3. Now, I'll ask you just once more. Coat off. No? Right that's your C4. I'll get on-call and you can leave.'

In this case, the adult has decided before the lesson that he does not like the child and in doing so weaponises the child's own defiance against him. The C system has become a trap door for the young person, who then disappears from view. You can bet that the teacher will not visit the resulting detention to attempt any kind of repair, and then the whole carry-on gets repeated next time and the time after that. The C system discourages staff from building relationships. Most pupils will not need to be involved with it, and the minority who do will find the teacher's refusal to engage enraging.

These pyramids often lead to full corridors, overflowing behaviour provision and stressed-out pastoral teams. And, in some schools, a certain cohort simply leave, unable to cope with a regime that will not listen and simply reflects their own alienation back at them. They go somewhere else.

If your school has a C system and you are forced to work within it, here are some pointers:

- Do not fall into the trap of thinking it will 'sort behaviour'. There is always more to do.

- Build relationships with all your pupils, especially those whose behaviour is not always great.

- If you set a detention, go to it. Speak to the child and attempt a repair and rebuild conversation.

- Think about the steps you can take before you hand out a C1. What might you add in – a quiet word? A non-verbal signal? Friendly encouragement?

- Simple directions and reminders teach the behaviours you want to see, whereas the C system treats your kids like cattle bumping into an electrified fence. You will not have a happy herd.

- Deliver your reminders as privately as possible to maintain the pupil's dignity and the positive nature of your lesson.

'I'm very disappointed'

Back at Ilford County High, a new maths teacher arrived in Year 9: Mr Terrell. He was different to the others. Unlike every other maths teacher we'd had, when we misbehaved for Mr Terrell he did not get angry, he did not raise his voice and he did not turn puce. He just became disappointed. It was extremely powerful. His disappointment told us that he thought better of us. Quite honestly, we were used to being told that we were useless and very, very bad. For someone to come out and tell us that he thought highly of us and we were letting ourselves down was quite striking. As a result, misbehaviour was very much the exception in Mr Terrell's lesson.

I have written elsewhere in this book about the 95% and the 5%. When we teach, we differentiate, and the same is true when we give consequences. Consistency is the holy grail, quite rightly, in schools, but please do not confuse it with uniformity. Each pupil has risk factors (for example, the parents have split up or dad is long-term unemployed) and they also have some resilience factors (for example, a warm, loving grandma or a big sister who looks out for them). Each child will have a unique mix of risk and resilience factors, and so it is nonsense to say, as some staff do, 'Well, *her* parents split up and *she* doesn't misbehave!' without knowing what resilience factors have supported this child to succeed.

'Make the right choice'

For many pupils, the language of choice is a reasonable tack to take. When the average pupil is caught bang to rights with their phone in a lesson, and is initially unwilling to hand it over à la the school policy, the teacher might well say, 'You need to make the right choice here, Tony.' Tony can think through the consequences of handing over the phone and those of refusal, and he can make some kind of informed judgement about where the greatest pain and inconvenience probably lies.

However, our 5% are acting out the trauma of adverse childhood experiences; they struggle to regulate their emotions because their brains have not developed as they might have done. Expecting them to 'make the right choice' is quite futile. 'You know the rule' or 'You know the expectation/routine' is a much better route to take, as you are appealing to a learned habit rather than a sophisticated assessment of future consequences.

Certainty, not severity

If you need to keep a child back, use the time to make your point (they need to know that the behaviour was not acceptable), listen to their side of the story/explanation, get to know them and show you have a human side.

Think about making the consequence fit the crime too. If the behaviour harmed the learning of the class, what can this child do in reparation – perhaps help you to tidy a shelf or prepare a resource? If they missed the work, they might be expected to make up for it before tomorrow.

The certainty of the consequence – that if you say you will keep them back, you make it happen – is far more important than its severity. You should also insist that they behave well during their time with you. The length of the conversation should reflect very clearly the quality of the pupil's engagement in it. As we saw in Chapter 1, restorative conversations are crucial when building trust in relationships.

The big picture

Rewards and consequences need to be part of a holistic approach. If you have not thought through how you are teaching behaviour and how praise, rewards and consequences fit into that, you are likely to confuse and confound your audience.

I was watching a young teacher lead a personal, social, health and citizenship education lesson with his Year 8 form recently. His approach seemed fundamentally confused. Here are some excerpts from my notes to him:

> You mentioned that you were looking forward to giving rewards, which was great, but then you told them that 'I don't want to be giving out sanctions' and 'Don't make me give them out.' A couple of things occur to me about this:

- You introduced the idea of poor behaviour when you did not need to. This gave away the fact that your expectations for this group were low, and so the class decided to live up to your damning assessment.

- When you say, 'I don't want to give out sanctions,' you risk coming over as someone who is willing to be pushed and pushed before you will act. I am not suggesting you go wild with the consequences, but if you make promises – positive or negative – you must keep them, otherwise you will not seem credible or trustworthy.

- At the end of the session you gave out stamps and behaviour points. There is some value in this, but by waiting until the end of the lesson, you lost any effect they might have had on today's lesson. Suppose that, part way through, you stopped and handed out some behaviour points for all those who had engaged by that point? This would have encouraged the others to get on board. If any of those you praise goes on to misbehave, you have the good example to work with: 'Donna? Earlier this lesson I praised you for your concentration. That's the Donna I need to see right now, thanks.'

This young man was presenting mixed messages and, consequently, the class did not engage with him as they might have.

Restorative approaches

Some teachers want revenge after a behaviour incident. A young person has shown them disrespect and they want them punished; they might even refuse to teach the pupil concerned until they get their pound of flesh.

A restorative approach says, 'I am the adult in this situation. The child is learning to behave, and right now they are getting it very wrong. I am still their teacher. I do not need revenge; I just need them to engage with me so they can learn.' Restorative approaches are a mindset.

If you search online for 'restorative questions', you will find a list similar to this one:

- What happened?

- What were you thinking at the time?

- What have you thought since?

- Who was harmed by what happened?

- What do you think should happen now?

These are useful questions, but they are not the last word on restorative practice. I will content myself here by saying that if you accept that nothing the child does will divest you of your responsibility to teach them, and you make their learning your sole aim, you will be working in a restorative manner.

There are two ways of teaching pupils to behave. You can do it by reaching for the extrinsic motivation of rewards and sanctions, or you can do it intrinsically through relationships and routines. I have outlined ways to cope with behaviourist systems in this chapter because they are so prevalent in our schools, but your priority must be to motivate pupils through teaching really well, building great relationships with them and establishing routines that make positive behaviours automatic.

Takeaways

- Make sure you acknowledge the good behaviours that you have told the class you want to see.

- Avoid creating elaborate rewards systems. If you invest in good relationships with your pupils, then doing the right thing will be its own reward.

- Praise works best if it is merited, specific and awarded within the context of a rewarding relationship.

- Sometimes a consequence needs to be applied, but keep in mind that this alone will not fix the situation.

- Certainty is far more important than severity.

NOW TRY THIS:

Record your lesson. Video is best but audio will do. Count the number of times you talk about good behaviour and the number of times you talk about bad behaviour. What do your findings tell you?

Chapter 9

CAUSES

When I was at teacher training college in the mid-1980s, our lecturers told us that if we were simply kind and engaging and taught great lessons, then pupils would inevitably behave like angels. Sadly, although these aspects of our professionalism are indispensable, the advice I was given is not the whole truth. Rudolf Dreikurs (1897–1972), an Austrian psychiatrist working in Chicago, came up with four 'mistaken goals' that children are aiming at when they misbehave.[1] It is a model that has always rung true when I have thought about the pupils I come across who persistently get it wrong.

Mistaken goal number 1: undue attention

We have all met the child whose behaviour seems to scream 'Notice me!' They shout out constantly, crawl about on the floor and do stuff that is too daft to describe, all in pursuit of keeping your attention. All four goals are about belonging, but this child believes that 'I only count when I have your attention.' Addressing this takes a concerted effort to find the child behaving appropriately and showering them with attention then. You will hear pupils described in the staffroom as 'attention-seeking'; I think a more helpful description is 'connection-seeking'. The child appears to seek meaningless attention when what they need is meaningful connection.

There were many excellent ideas in the SEAL materials and what follows is one of my favourites. When a child (up until the age of about 12) keeps interrupting you, you might try making three 'golden tokens' – perhaps coins made out of cardboard and sprayed gold. 'Here are three golden tokens,' you say to the child. 'You can interrupt me three times in this session, but each time you do so, you need to give me one of these tokens. When your last token is used, you can't interrupt any more.' It is a great way to help young people become more self-aware, which is the first step on the road to self-control.

---

1   Rudolf Dreikurs, *Psychology in the Classroom: A Manual for Teachers* (New York: Harper & Row, 1968).

Mistaken goal number 2: undue power

'I only count when I'm in control' is a belief that leads to a whole lot of trouble. These children will dig their heels in, meeting your instructions with 'No!' or 'You can't make me!' You will have heard that giving a child who struggles to behave some responsibility is a useful tactic. The mistaken quest for power is the reason why. They can be book monitor, board monitor or some other helpful role.

I have stressed elsewhere the importance of stating established rules and routines. If you want the class to listen to Emily's contribution, and Jake continues chatting, you might say, 'Jake, be quiet now; it is Emily's turn to speak.' Jake might decide that you have picked him out to boss him around and he would rather have his own way, so he keeps chatting and ignoring your instruction. Suppose, instead, when it is Emily's turn to speak, you simply announce, 'One voice, thank you.' You are reminding the whole class of an established routine, and the situation is no longer about a battle of wills between you and Jake but a statement about 'the way we do things here'.

Giving these children choices is another harmless way to let them wield just a little power. The child who refuses to join any group and will not back down can be given a choice: 'You can join the red group or the blue group; it's up to you.' The child now feels they have some control and begins to learn the art of compromise.

Mistaken goal number 3: revenge

This child is hurt because they do not feel they belong, and now they want revenge on those who do. These children can be so hurtful to others that it is easy to overlook that *they* are hurting. The mantra here is 'connection before correction'. These children need to hear the message that you are not going anywhere and cannot be driven away. Working with these children requires leaving your ego and your sense of fairness at the door. You need to be prepared to look deep below the surface.

If, as I have said elsewhere, behaviour is a form of communication, the behaviour motivated by a desire for revenge can be the toughest language to translate. They need to hear explicitly that they belong more times than we might believe is necessary, and they need to feel it implicitly too in the way in which the whole school behaves towards them. If we insist that they attend a unit called 'Inclusion' that sits at the far end of the school field, we are sending a mixed message. Think about the looks that these children receive from adults in school. Disapproval does not work, but watching staff interact with children, I sometimes wonder if they have read the memo.

Mistaken goal number 4: assumed inadequacy

There is no more dispiriting sight than the child who has their head on the desk. Where to start? This child has decided that they only belong when they are helpless and need rescuing. You can waste ages pleading with and cajoling them. Small steps, gentle encouragement and, above all, emotional consistency are key. If you state gently that you are here to help one minute and threaten dire consequences the next, this child will not trust you and you will get nowhere. Behaviour like this should be referred up, so the school has a clear picture and more digging can be done, if needed.

Because they are kids!

We need reminding sometimes that children are, well, children. They are by definition immature. This leads to a number of difficulties.

Firstly, it means that pupils will make mistakes. They will push boundaries and experiment with different versions of themselves – or, to put it another way, they will try it on. If we are weak, so boundaries are not immediately felt, they will keep pushing. If we are repressive, they will begin to believe that their rebel pose is justified and behave accordingly.

Secondly, it makes respect problematic. Children tend to value things that seem pointless to us: celebrity culture, being cool, *Call of Duty*, the latest pop idol, TV talent shows, revolting snacks and sugary drinks, farting, having thousands of 'friends' on social media sites and staying in bed until teatime. Respecting people whose personal obsessions and cultural diet are radically different to your own is an issue for some adults in schools. If half the items on that list sound appealing to you, by the way, that is great; you will have a head start when you need to connect.

Before we get too self-righteous about the immature behaviour of our pupils, it is worth observing the behaviour of the average teacher on a CPD day. There is something about wearing jeans and trainers in the workplace that seems to bring out the worst in teachers. They arrive to sessions late while chatting and brandishing mugs of coffee, they text surreptitiously, they wander off task during activities, they interrupt and berate the trainer if they do not like the message, and they leave the room without explanation. In fact, they indulge in all the behaviours that would send them into an apoplectic rage if pupils did them in their lessons!

Of course, some of this behaviour is not so bad. It is just what comes naturally in certain situations – for example, it is quite natural to talk to other people when you are in an audience. It is said that we should 'tighten up to be good … loosen to become outstanding'.[2] How about loosening by abandoning the draconian 'no-talking' rule as pupils enter assembly? If they respond quickly to a signal for silence at the start of proceedings, what exactly is gained by having them file in silently like extras from *The Handmaid's Tale*?

As a young teacher in assembly, standing at the side of the year group, I sometimes found it very hard to stay onside while the head of lower school tore into pupils who had the temerity to speak to the person next to them before the assembly had begun. The eye-popping tirade that ensued and the air of repression that followed did not help any of our visiting speakers promote their various causes.

Because of what is happening to their brains

Molly Edmonds of HowStuffWorks uses the metaphor of a home stereo system to describe the way in which the brain reshapes itself during adolescence:

> Think of the teenage brain as an entertainment centre that hasn't been fully hooked up. There are loose wires, so that the speaker system isn't working with the DVD player, which in turn hasn't been

---

2   Peter Dougill, Mike Raleigh, Roy Blatchford, Lyn Fryer, Carol Robinson and John Richmond, *To the Next Level: Good Schools Becoming Outstanding. Research Report* (Reading: CfBT Education Trust, 2011), p. 15. Available at: https://www.educationdevelopmenttrust.com/EducationDevelopmentTrust/files/89/89fc7659-9fd4-448e-a0f6-df548565bd02.pdf.

formatted to work with the television yet. And ... the remote control hasn't even arrived![3]

As an adult, the planning and delivery of your lesson will be dominated by your prefrontal cortex, which allows you to judge the impact of your actions, weigh up the pros and cons of different decisions and so on. This impulse control system is situated near the front of your brain. Guess what? Teenage thinking takes place at the back of the brain. The most developed, and therefore most dominant, part of the teenage brain is the nucleus accumbens, an area which registers pleasure and reward. So, while a mature adult brain might be compared to a diplomatic residence, the teenage brain is more akin to Las Vegas. Combine an underdeveloped impulse control system with an exaggerated hunger for pleasure and reward ... and you have a recipe for typical teenage behaviour.

It would be really nice if, at the start of the lesson, young people thought about me in this way: 'He seems a good bloke, and I need to work hard for that exam in three years' time, so I'd better sit attentively through these poems because, if I do well in my exam, I may be a successful professional by my mid-twenties.' Unfortunately, the teenage brain, a teeming hoard of hedonistic impulses with no police force, merely thinks, 'Ha! It's not a proper teacher! No work for us today! We can have some fun at this guy's expense.'

It is not that they will not choose to be good in situations where the usual rules seem not to apply; often they literally cannot. Or, at least, those who have been raised by parents who tend to be impulsive and fail to model good decision-making will certainly fail this test. The plasticity of the brain means that impulse control can be learned but only if it is observed, practised and rewarded from an early age. Plus, those whose upbringing has not been nurturing will probably lack empathy, so do not expect them to care if others' learning is affected.

---

3   Molly Edmonds, Are Teenage Brains Really Different from Adult Brains?, *HowStuffWorks* (26 August 2008). Available at: https://science.howstuffworks.com/life/inside-the-mind/human-brain/teenage-brain1.htm.

Because you talk too much

Remember your school days? Watching the minute hand of the classroom wall clock refuse to budge? What bores you now? Somebody droning on about a dull subject does it for me. If they are reading their PowerPoint slides that magnifies the effect. If they are the fourth or fifth person to do this on the day in question, the effect is multiplied exponentially. If they use words I do not understand, I switch off completely and … And if, all this time, they are telling me about stuff I already know, then my next public statement might be made from the dock, entering a plea of diminished responsibility.

When I worked for a local authority, the training days were torture. We would sit in the large room and, one by one, colleagues would stand up and speak in great detail about their own line of work. It was how I imagine government working in the old Soviet Union: 'Comrade Baker will now inform us about the progress of the five-year plan to improve the production of small and medium-sized widgets.'

These presentations were either accompanied with densely populated PowerPoint slides or there was nothing to focus on but the individual standing in front of us. We were an education department, for heaven's sake; could we not think up a better way of sharing information or a more imaginative way of structuring training days? Common estimates for sustained attention to a freely chosen task range from about five minutes for a 2-year-old child to a maximum of around twenty minutes in older children and adults.[4] And that is a freely chosen task. Imagine how much the attention suffers when we did not ask to do the task in the first place.

Schools also underestimate the effect of a sequence of lessons presented to a pupil over a full day. If at 2pm a teenager, with her barely functioning impulse control system, is given her fourth textbook of the day from which to take notes in silence, it is no surprise if she behaves poorly. In some teachers' estimation, it is the children who can put up with this predicament who are the 'good kids' and those who cannot are the 'bad kids', thus without really meaning to we are separating the wheat from the chaff on the basis of their attention span, which seems very unfair, especially when

---

4   David Cornish and Dianne Dukette, *The Essential 20: Twenty Components of an Excellent Health Care Team* (Pittsburgh, PA: RoseDog Books, 2009), p. 73.

you take into consideration conditions such as attention deficit disorder and attention deficit hyperactivity disorder, which make concentration really, really hard.

Because some children have unmet special educational or additional needs

Children with additional needs need your routine more. You must know about and plan for pupils who have a diagnosis, for those who have one pending and for those who may not have the badge but definitely have the behaviour. When these children's behaviour requires a response, intensify rather than escalate. Punishing them will be ineffective and, if you think about it, pretty abhorrent. They need more care and more structure.

There is a wealth of advice on teaching children with additional needs on the internet – for example, the Special Needs Jungle.[5] There are plenty of excellent books available too, such as *The Teacher's Guide to SEN* by Natalie Packer.[6] Your special needs and disabilities coordinator (or additional learning needs coordinator) should be able to help. They will be nothing but thrilled to discover that a teacher cares enough to approach them and ask for guidance.

Because of unstructured time

It is said that the devil makes work for idle hands. A saying never truer than in the classroom. Watching new teachers go about their business, one of the first jobs I do is to help them eliminate unstructured time. Hands become idle when your lesson is interrupted, so your job, via thorough preparation, is to foresee threats to the flow of your lesson and head them off at the pass. These unstructured moments are fatal to a good lesson, and can often be ruled out with a bit of planning and forethought.

---

5   See, for example, Renata Blower, Top Teaching Tips for Children with SEND, *Special Needs Jungle* (17 February 2021). Available at: https://www.specialneedsjungle.com/top-teaching-tips-for-children-with-send.
6   Natalie Packer, *The Teacher's Guide to SEN* (Carmarthen: Crown House Publishing, 2017).

Imagine the scene: John is teaching English to a class of 13-year-olds. He has just done the register when a pupil arrives late. John breaks off from his introduction to reprimand the latecomer, who claims to have been to the toilet. John is drawn into a dispute about this, and the class, lacking an explanation of the starter activity displayed on the board, fall to chatting among themselves. He then notices that three pupils are not in their correct seats according to his seating plan. Three minutes is lost arguing the toss with these pupils.

John begins to explain the starter activity and is interrupted by a member of pastoral staff: 'Sorry to interrupt, sir. Do you remember I asked you for some work for Kerry? She is working in isolation today.' Another two minutes while John grabs a textbook and some A4 paper and scribbles some instructions on the paper. During this time, several pupils leave their chairs and wander about to chat with friends. Others doodle and one or two begin heated arguments. John motions for the pupils to return to their seats. Ten minutes have passed now and he has got nowhere. He begins again, only this time a bright spark on the back row points out a spelling mistake in the PowerPoint slide. While he leans over the PC to correct his typo, one boy in row three thumps the boy next to him, who dives to the floor in mock agony. This is going to be a long day.

I am sure you can see what has happened here: a lack of planning and communication. All of these interruptions could have been anticipated and planned for. A routine for latecomers, the work for Kerry, a carefully written PowerPoint slide and vigilance about who goes to what seat at the start of the hour would have eliminated the unstructured time and improved behaviour immeasurably.

Because of a lack of boundaries

I spoke about boundaries in Chapter 5, as they are an important part of making a lasting connection. They are also vital for leading behaviour effectively – a lesson I learned during my first experience of teaching.

While I was considering my career path at the age of about 20, my dad, who was a primary school caretaker, somehow persuaded the head teacher to let me take a class one afternoon. I had thirty 10-year-olds all to myself for two hours. Sadly, I do not remember the content. What I do remember was that, having given them the task, I very quickly found myself confronted with a queue that snaked all the way around the classroom. There was hardly anyone sitting working; they were all in line waiting to show me their work. These delightful children were not being naughty, they were simply doing what came naturally; because I had not set a boundary, they did not see one.

I had made the classic mistake of assuming they would know what I wanted. What did I want? I wanted them to stay seated unless called to join me at my desk. I also wanted them to review and revise their own work before asking for me to mark it. However, I had not thought to tell them. This was, no doubt about it, a lovely class of likeable and enthusiastic individuals who were hungry for knowledge. My lack of boundaries turned them into a disorderly rabble in five minutes.

The chances are that someone has given you this advice: 'Don't smile until Christmas.' This is completely unhelpful. The right smile communicates confidence and self-assurance. So long as you have 'the look' to fall back on (see Chapter 2), there is no harm whatsoever in smiling. I have known some teachers wear glasses just so they can look over the top of them, and keep looking for a moment longer in a way that says gently, 'That's enough.'

There is a grain of truth in there, which is this: do not aim to be your pupils' friend. They need a kind, empathetic adult, not a friend. It is also true that there are many different kinds of smile and not all would be appropriate. Some are gushing, or fake, or fawning. Your smile should say, 'I am pleased to be here, I am pleased to be in your company and I am looking forward to the lesson.' No more than that.

Because of poor literacy

When you use the whiteboard, how large is your font? It needs to be easily visible to all. What resources do you use, and what level of reading skills do they require? Your special educational needs coordinator will be very happy to look at your materials to make sure they are accessible. When I carry out pupil voice activities I routinely ask, 'What makes a good teacher?' and they nearly always reply, 'They help you when you're stuck.' You can work proactively to keep your pupils unstuck by checking that they can access your lesson. Think about the vocabulary that you use too. You might think your explanation of cloud types or simple division is crystal clear, but if you have used words your class are not familiar with then they will not get it.

Have you ever struggled with a set of instructions that were impossible to follow? On our kitchen worktop at home, Sian and I have one of those digital devices that displays pictures of the family on rotation and answers us when we want to know what the weather will be like on Tuesday. Living in rural Wales, we were only recently upgraded to full fibre broadband, so there is a new router in the corner of the room. You would think that connecting this machine to a new network would be a simple matter. Think again. After an hour of struggling with a task that was beyond my comprehension, I was just about ready to commit murder. Sian had a grumpy husband on her hands for a few minutes. Luckily she is used to that.

It is no wonder that children who cannot read or understand what is being said behave badly. The link is well established: '70% of pupils permanently excluded from school have difficulties in basic literacy skills. 25% of young offenders are said to have reading skills below those of the average 7-year-old. 60% of the prison population is said to have difficulties in basic literacy skills.'[7] Most pupils will not volunteer that they are struggling; many will keep their heads down and quietly fail if we let them. Others, frustrated and angry – just as I was in the kitchen the other day, will become disruptive, aggressive and antisocial. This should not be a surprise.

One of the reasons I am so opposed to draconian punishments is the disproportionate number of pupils with special needs among detention and exclusion data. In fact, children with special needs and disabilities (SEND) account for almost two-thirds of exclusions.[8] It is a scandal. Children are set up to fail if their unmet needs put them on a conveyor belt, via poor behaviour and exclusion, all the way into prison. Why does this happen? I could bang on about causes such as underinvestment in education and the damage that a damning Ofsted judgement can do to a school, but this is not that book. I will simply say that you can make a difference by ensuring

7   Christina Clark and George Dugdale, *Literacy Changes Lives: The Role of Literacy in Offending Behaviour. A Discussion Piece* (London: National Literacy Trust, 2008), p. 6. Available at: https://cdn.literacytrust.org.uk/media/documents/2008_11_15_free_research_-_Literacy_changes_lives_2008_offending_behaviour_JYS9ScS.pdf.
8   See https://www.goodschoolsguide.co.uk/special-educational-needs/your-rights/school-exclusions.

that the pupils you teach are able to read what you put in front of them and understand what you say.

Children misbehave for all kinds of reasons, and I hope you will agree that it has been interesting to consider them for a while in this chapter. Certainly, we can understand the need to belong as a key motivator for some of the misbehaviour we see. However, most of the time we are better off taking a solution-focused approach. Rather than analysing the problem behaviours, we can ask ourselves, 'What behaviours do I want instead?' Teaching those behaviours, as described in Chapters 4 and 6, is the best response.

Takeaways

- Children's inappropriate behaviour is often motivated by their need to belong. If you can enable them to feel they belong in your lesson, you are halfway there.

- Avoid unstructured time if at all possible. The devil really does make work for idle hands.

- Be aware of the effect of poor literacy. Are your resources and your teaching methods accessible to all your pupils?

- Children are children. We should not be surprised when they behave in an immature way or test our boundaries.

NOW TRY THIS:

Think about a lesson you are going to teach next week. What potential causes of inappropriate behaviour can you predict and plan for?

Chapter 10

REFLECTIONS

Thank you for sticking with me thus far. Before we call it a day, I feel I need to answer this question: how on earth did I get from where I started to where I am now? Somehow, I went from blaming the kids for their behaviour to teaching them to behave. It was a series of lessons learned over time. Here are some of the key points I absorbed along the way, and I list them here to sum up the core messages in this book:

- You need to teach good lessons with clear routines if you want the 95% to behave.

- You must build relationships with the 5% if you want them to behave.

- You must teach the exact behaviours you want to see, model them in your own behaviour and highlight them when you see them.

- You need to take responsibility for behaviour in your own room by doing your own follow-up conversations. Punishment alone will not work.

- You get more of what you notice, so catch them being good.

- Children are people with a valid point of view. We must show respect first.

- Never value your content more than your audience.

- Children crave the company of stable, resilient adults. Act that way until you feel it.

- You are not there to give children what you think they deserve, but to help them find what they need.

- Life is short and the first lesson every day must be that it is good to be alive. Look like you want to be there.

How did I come to adopt these ideas? It is fashionable these days to say you have been on a journey. Certainly, if you had sat down next to me, tearfully smoking in the staffroom at Stocksbridge, and told me I would be writing this book one day – *and* getting it published – I might have laughed (or more likely coughed) at you. But here I am, and here you are reading it. If I have been on a journey, it has been a mystery tour; I am not one of those people who sets a goal and kills his own granny to get there. You will not find me on *The Apprentice* any time soon.

What I can lay claim to is a willingness to reflect. I often hear senior leaders praise individual staff with, 'She's a reflective practitioner,' which to me suggests a dentist wrapped in kitchen foil. But there is something in this. There are those who, when taking part in training, reflect on their own practice, tweak it and make progress, and there are those who, although they sit nodding sagely throughout the morning, see no need to alter their own practice. They are missing a trick. For whatever reason, I have been able to reflect, to imagine a better way and to move in that direction. There have been pivotal moments and pivotal people.

For example, I was lucky that it was John who found me in the staffroom on that dreadful day when I had walked out on my Year 9 drama class. When John and his lovely partner, Denise, stayed over one weekend, he bought, planned and cooked our Saturday night meal before I could raise a finger to object. I was benignly brushed aside and, not being the competitive sort, I let him get on with it. So, John was exactly the right person to find me in that sorry state; he had the balls to take me back to room D9, sit me down and show me how it was done. To my credit, I did not bristle. I sat and learned.

Another moment to cherish is that training day in Leeds with Bill Rogers back in 1993. I had the strangest reaction to his message. It seemed shockingly new, and yet it also seemed like I had known it all along. It was acutely enlightening, and it was also simple common sense. The Australian reminded me of Muhammad Ali, the legendary 'Greatest of All Time', who would, they say, hit you with a shot which barely made contact that it almost tickled you, but then, in the blink of an eye, the next one would slam in like a sledgehammer, leaving you prone and winded on the canvas. Bill Rogers opened my mind with his hilarious comedy, and then sent me reeling with a stern moral challenge. It is a style I have done my best to imitate ever since.

I am also forever indebted to the girl with the crisps. It was her question, 'Why didn't you just ask for one?' that led me to see this was not a game. My pupils were more than problems to be managed or an audience to entertain; they were people with feelings and a valid point of view. The taste of cheese and onion soon faded, replaced by a hunger for showing and receiving respect. It is an addictive and hugely enjoyable activity which many staff deny themselves because they would rather blame the kids.

Mrs Baines is another pivotal character on my journey. I am glad that I chose not to be defensive or indignant, that I listened to what she said and heard it for what it was – a wake-up call. From that day forward, I saw the importance of my own behaviour. I learned a great deal at parents' evenings. Of course, there are one or two whose parents do not ever show up and those whose parenting leaves much to be desired, but many of our pupils, who we might be tempted to see as little pains, have parents who love them just as much as our parents loved us. Becoming a parent helps in this regard: when you send your flesh and blood off to school, and you consider how you would like your little ones to be treated, it brings home the responsibility that teaching entails.

And, as I keep saying, I did not always get it right. During my stint as a head of year, I once asked a boy who had come to school in an oversized pair of black shorts why he was dressed as Popeye. That lunchtime, I was called to the phone in the staffroom. I picked up the receiver and a menacing voice intoned, 'It's Popeye's dad here.' The excruciating conversation that followed was all I needed to remind me that respect was everything, and I needed to keep my sense of humour in check.

Another aspect of my character that I needed to keep in check was my temper. I can thank a boy called David for that. David was in trouble from the moment he joined us in Year 7. He was a chubby child with a flat face, a tendency to bully other children and, on at least one occasion, a liking for whiskey. Goodness knows how it came into his possession but he polished off a small bottle. Half cut and slurring, David was placed in a side office where he sat loudly snoring while the SLT decided what to do with him. Once the decision and the accompanying phone calls had been made, someone had the misfortune to open the door, at which point it became clear that David's snoring had only served to drown out his farting. The stench was incredible. If anyone had lit a match, we would have been blown to kingdom come.

Anyway, a couple of years later, by 3.30pm, I was at the end of my tether. I'd had just about enough of David's constant breaking of any rule he came across. I do not remember what he had done this time or why it triggered me, but this time was one time too many ... and out there on the empty corridor, perhaps ten minutes after home time, I blew. Big time. I screamed, I yelled, I gave him both barrels, reloaded and gave him more. It was the most out-of-control bollocking I ever gave anyone, and I am ashamed to think of it now.

To make things even worse, I had forgotten that David's mother was a cleaner at the school and she was busy scrubbing tables in the next room. Looking back, she was remarkably restrained; all I can remember is her telling me about her husband's heart condition. David was unmoved, his mother was in tears and I looked a complete prat. Never again. I was pleased the following year to visit David at his work experience placement and further pleased to praise him for the positive things his employers said about him. That was a lesson in itself. Some people simply are not suited to school. Just because a young person fails to succeed in school, this does not mean they will not succeed in life.

Eventually, I grew into the role of head of year. I came to see myself as the pastor of a secular flock and, despite the firefighting aspect of the job, I loved it. Then local authorities began to appoint behaviour and attendance consultants.

Since attending Bill Rogers' training, I had built up a modest CV by sharing his methods with other teachers and support staff, and I was lucky to be appointed to one of these behaviour and attendance roles with Wakefield Council. Working for a local authority was another steep learning curve, like one of those rollercoasters when you think you have experienced the stiffest challenge but the next turn is faster and harder still. After a wobbly start, I made a decent fist of it (that seems to be a pattern with me) and I found myself in line for a much bigger job with the National Strategies, which was basically a government role. As a regional adviser in Yorkshire and the Humber, it was my job to support and challenge local authorities to meet certain targets by reducing exclusions and increasing attendance. Let us just say it taught me how to handle difficult conversations. Since the National Strategies ended, I have been a freelance consultant, coach and trainer.

I was looking for new opportunities one day when I was told about Paul Dix. I got in touch and Paul was kind enough to invite me to a school in Luton where he would be delivering a half day's training. Another pivotal moment. It was just like being in the room with Bill Rogers twenty-three years earlier. Paul was funny, brilliant and compelling. I can only compare it to that moment at Christmas when the family is sat around doing a jigsaw puzzle and someone fits the last piece in place. The whole picture comes alive. Paul had an analysis and a plan that made sense to me. I drove home to Yorkshire with my brain on fire and now, seven years later, I am proud to be part of Paul's team at When the Adults Change.

I gave a talk at Huddersfield University once to about 200 trainee teachers. As I was packing away, one of them bounded up to me and asked, 'How do I get to be you?' Taken aback, I could only tell her that she should be careful what she wished for, but then I added, more seriously, 'There is no route map, but when your bus comes, get on it.'

Some teachers are affronted when told that pupil behaviour is their responsibility, but in fact it is a liberating message because, if the kids' behaviour was all their own fault, how could you change it? Once you see the power of your own behaviour, you have a route to a better place. They will change when you do.

If you are finding behaviour hard to lead, I hope I have given you some useful strategies, and I hope you will take heart from the fact that this stuff can be learned. You may not be there yet, but with practice, reflection and courage, and with the support of colleagues, you can succeed.

BEHAVIOUR CHECKLIST

There are many actions you can take to improve the behaviour of your classes.

This checklist features some of them. You can use it to chart your progress as you make your way through this book.

Do you ...?

	Not yet	Partly	Yes
Plan for behaviour.			
Invest time in establishing routines and high expectations.			
Invest time in building relationships.			
Address the small things – chewing, leaning on chairs, etc.			
Ignore secondary behaviours.			
Meet and greet pupils every lesson.			
Use specific, targeted and tactical praise to motivate individuals.			
Use a signal for attention.			

	Not yet	Partly	Yes
Apply, and stick to, a routine for how pupils gain my attention.			
Demonstrate boundaries.			
Adopt confident, positive body language and smile.			
Remind classes exactly how I want them to behave.			
Show respect to all pupils unconditionally.			
Highlight good behaviour more than bad behaviour.			
Manage my own feelings – remaining the adult.			
Keep my emotions separate from pupil behaviour.			
Separate the behaviour from the child.			

PUPIL SURVEY

Use this survey to find out how pupils feel about being in your lesson. What actions will you take in response to your findings? Run the survey again next term and see how your actions have improved pupil engagement.

	Strongly agree	Agree	Neither agree nor disagree	Disagree	Strongly disagree
1. I enjoy our lessons.					
2. My teacher is fair.					
3. I know what the rules are.					
4. If I work hard and behave, I get noticed.					
5. The class behaves well.					
6. Poor behaviour is managed effectively.					
7. My teacher keeps their promises.					
8. The work is not too hard or too easy.					
9. I feel safe in our lessons.					
10. My teacher will help me if I have a problem.					

MODELLING SELF-REVIEW ACTIVITY

Record a time during the week when you are seen to model each of these qualities. Note how your pupils respond. As you make your way through the book, come back to the survey and repeat it, perhaps once a term during the year. What has changed?

Self-awareness	
Empathy	
Managing feelings	
Kindness	
Openness	
Motivation	
Social skills	
Humility	
Patience	
Other	

RESPONDING TO LOW-LEVEL DISRUPTION

This is not an exhaustive list, but it contains some of the more helpful phrases that you might use to get better responses from pupils when you need to address their behaviour.

Highlight those who are getting it right:

- 'Well done this group – you've all got your books out ready to learn.'
- 'Thank you, Jake, for listening ... Thank you, Sarah, for listening ...'

Describe what you see:

- 'Jake, you are out of your chair.'

Give a simple direction:

- 'I need you to sit down.'

Assume compliance:

- (*After the direction*) ... thank you.'

Describe what you need to see:

- 'Jason ... (*pause*) ... looking this way, thanks.'
- 'Shareen ... (*pause*) ... taking the coat off, thanks.'

Fogging:

- 'I hear what you say ... taking the coat off, thanks.'
- 'Maybe she is talking to you ... looking this way, thanks.'

Rule reminder:

- 'One voice, thank you.'
- 'Jason ... (*pause*) ... what is the rule about shouting out?'
- 'Shareen ... (*pause*) ... what is the rule about coats?'

Consequence reminder:

- 'Jason … (*pause*) … what will happen if you keep shouting out?'

(And if the pupil's reply indicates a bad choice: 'So are you choosing to …?')

- 'Sunhil … (*pause*) … what will happen if you keep your coat on?'

(And if the pupil's reply indicates a bad choice: 'So are you choosing to …?)

Tell the class *explicitly* and *relentlessly* what you want – for example:

- 'I need pens down, mouths closed and eyes on me, thank you.'

COMMON SITUATIONS REQUIRING ROUTINES AND PROTOCOLS

Situation	What happens in my classroom?	How effective? Less _____ more					Action
		1	2	3	4	5	
Entering the room							
Taking the register							
Collecting homework							
Gaining the attention of the class							
Transition between activities							
Lack of equipment							

Situation	What happens in my classroom?	How effective? Less _____ more					Action
		1	2	3	4	5	
Pupils arriving late							
Questioning							
Requests to leave the class							
Packing away							
Leaving the room							

LESSON REVIEW

We will leave an in-depth account of Ofsted-friendly teaching for another book. For now, I will limit myself to asking some simple questions. I want you to think about the routine aspects of your teaching and whether they encourage learning.

1. Is the lesson memorable? Will it feature in a conversation one day where two of your ex-pupils reminisce over a pint? 'Do you remember when Mr Baker ...' Of course, by definition, not every lesson can be outstanding, but we can start with a puzzle, a challenge or a mystery – something to spark their interest.

2. Are the pupils busy? You might get pupils up to the whiteboard one by one to take part in your plenary, but is this an activity they could all be doing in pairs or small groups?

3. Are you checking out pupils' understanding? Get those whiteboards out so you get constant feedback.

4. Do you know the needs of all your learners? Pupils with SEND? What are literacy levels like? Who has an education, health and care plan?

5. How will learners demonstrate progress?

6. Have you consulted with your classes about the content and style of your lessons? Have you altered either as a result?

7. Are there opportunities to collaborate? If so, have you taught them how?

8. Does your questioning of pupils lead to higher level thinking?

9. Do you play tennis or basketball? That is, do you ask all the questions so that the 'ball' goes to and from you each time, or do you encourage pupils to question, develop and comment on each other's answers, so the 'ball' is passed around the room?

10. Do you talk too much?

REFERENCES

Blower, Renata (2021) Top Teaching Tips for Children with SEND, *Special Needs Jungle* (17 February). Available at: https://www.specialneedsjungle.com/top-teaching-tips-for-children-with-send.

Clark, Christina and Dugdale, George (2008) *Literacy Changes Lives: The Role of Literacy in Offending Behaviour. A Discussion Piece* (London: National Literacy Trust). Available at: https://cdn.literacytrust.org.uk/media/documents/2008_11_15_free_research_-_Literacy_changes_lives_2008_offending_behaviour_JYS9ScS.pdf.

Cornish, David and Dukette, Dianne (2009) *The Essential 20: Twenty Components of an Excellent Health Care Team* (Pittsburgh, PA: RoseDog Books).

Covey, Stephen R. (2017) *The 7 Habits of Highly Effective People: Powerful Lessons in Personal Change* (New York: Simon & Schuster).

Dix, Paul (2019) *When the Adults Change, Everything Changes* (Carmarthen: Independent Thinking Press).

Dix, Paul (2021) *After the Adults Change: Achievable Behaviour Nirvana* (Carmarthen: Independent Thinking Press).

Dougill, Peter; Raleigh, Mike; Blatchford, Roy; Fryer, Lyn; Robinson, Carol and Richmond, John (2011) *To the Next Level: Good Schools Becoming Outstanding. Research Report* (Reading: CfBT Education Trust). Available at: https://www.educationdevelopmenttrust.com/EducationDevelopmentTrust/files/89/89fc7659-9fd4-448e-a0f6-df548565bd02.pdf.

Dreikurs, Rudolf (1968) *Psychology in the Classroom: A Manual for Teachers* (New York: Harper & Row).

Dweck, Carol S. (2013) *Mindset: The New Psychology of Success* (New York: Ballantine).

Edmonds, Molly (2008) Are Teenage Brains Really Different from Adult Brains?, *HowStuffWorks* (26 August). Available at: https://science.howstuffworks.com/life/inside-the-mind/human-brain/teenage-brain1.htm.

Finnis, Mark (2021) *Restorative Practice* (Carmarthen: Independent Thinking Press).

Ginott, Haim G. (1972) *Teacher and Child: A Book for Parents and Teachers* (New York: Macmillan).

Goethe, Johann Wolfgang von (1824 [1796]) *Wilhelm Meister's Apprenticeship and Travels. Translated from the German of Goethe by Thomas Carlyle*, vol. 2 (London: Chapman and Hall).

Harris, Thomas (2012 [1967]) *I'm OK – You're OK: A Practical Guide to Transactional Analysis* (London: Arrow Press).

Lubenow, Gerald (1985) Rebel In My Soul, *Newsweek* (22 July).

O'Sullivan, James (2016) 80% Of All Communication is Non-Verbal, *Leap29* (27 May). Available at: https://www.leap29.com/blog/80-of-all-communication-is-no-verbal.

Packer, Natalie (2017) *The Teacher's Guide to SEN* (Carmarthen: Crown House Publishing).

Pierson, Rita F. (2013) Every Kid Needs a Champion [video], *TED*. Available at: https://www.ted.com/talks/rita_pierson_every_kid_needs_a_champion.

Rogers, Bill (1998) *You Know the Fair Rule: Strategies for Making the Hard Job of Discipline in Schools Easier*, 2nd edn (London: Pitman).

Rogers, Bill (2007) *Behaviour Management: A Whole-School Approach* (London: SAGE).

Wiliam, Dylan (2011) *Embedded Formative Assessment* (Bloomington, IN: Solution Tree Press).

ABOUT THE AUTHOR

Stephen Baker taught English and drama in Sheffield for seventeen years. After a spell with Wakefield Local Authority, he joined the National Strategies as a regional adviser for behaviour and attendance, before going on to become a freelance consultant. Stephen has written for a range of publications and his engaging style has made him a sought-after public speaker. An advocate of relational practice, before it had a name, Stephen has supported countless teaching staff with their classroom practice and senior leaders with their strategic leadership. He is passionate about helping new teachers establish themselves in the classroom and *That Behaviour Book* is a summation of his long career.

Stephen is a proud member of the When The Adults Change team and can be contacted via their website: www.whentheadultschange.com.

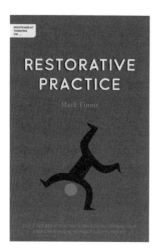

Independent Thinking on Restorative Practice
Building relationships, improving behaviour and creating stronger communities
Mark Finnis
ISBN: 978-178135338-7

For those educators who are uncomfortable with the punitive world of zero tolerance, isolation booths and school exclusions, Mark Finnis – one of the UK's leading restorative practice experts – is here to show you that there is another way.

Drawing on his many years' experience working with schools, social services and local governments across the country, Mark shares all you need to know about what restorative practice is, how it works, where to start and the many benefits of embedding a relational approach into any educational organisation that genuinely has people at its heart.

Covering coaching circles and the power of doing things with (and not to) children and young people, to moving your values off lanyards and posters and into the lived experience of every member of the school community, this book sets out how restorative practice – when done well – can transform every aspect of school life.

The book shares advice on how to put behaviour right when it goes wrong in a more positive, less punitive way, and, more importantly, on how to get it right and keep it right in the first place. Furthermore, it advocates an approach that is collaborative, empowering and positive – and ultimately geared to improve motivation, engagement and independent learning in even the hardest-to-reach young people.

Suitable for school leaders, educators and anyone working with young people.

The Kindness Principle

Making relational behaviour
management work in schools

Dave Whitaker

ISBN: 978-178135385-1

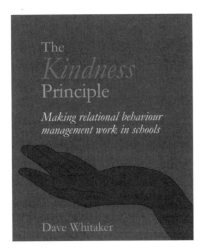

In an education system that too often reaches for the carrot-and-stick approach to dealing with poor pupil behaviour, an approach built on kindness and compassion might just provide the cure.

The Kindness Principle begins with the idea that relationships should be at the heart of behaviour management and culture, and sets out the ways in which the adoption of relational approaches can help create safer and happier schools. Schools where all staff and learners are valued and understood, where expectations and standards are high, and where kindness and acceptance matter.

Dave Whitaker explores why it is so important to understand children – offering techniques and advice on how to work effectively with all children (even the most challenging and troubled ones) without resorting to zero-tolerance, no-excuses and consequence-driven practices.

Dave also shares a wealth of real-life experiences from some of the most challenging schools in the country, along with research-informed insights that will help teachers understand children's behaviour in a new light. To this end he provides a wealth of guidance to help develop effective practice and learn from people who have actually walked the walk and don't just talk the talk.

Furthermore, the topics covered in the book include: restorative approaches, unconditional positive regard, building personal resilience, structures and routines, and the ins and outs of rewards and sanctions.

Suitable for teachers, school leaders and anyone working with children.

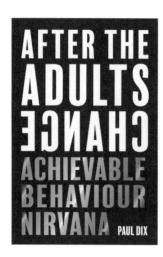

After The Adults Change
Achievable behaviour nirvana
Paul Dix
ISBN: 978-178135377-6

A revolution in behaviour can be exciting, dynamic and, at times, pleasantly terrifying. But revolution is short-lived. In this follow-up to his bestselling book *When the Adults Change, Everything Changes*, Paul Dix shows you that, after the behaviour of the adults has changed, there is an opportunity to go wider and deeper: to accelerate relational practice, decrease disproportionate punishment and fully introduce restorative, informed and coaching-led cultures.

Paul delves into the possibilities for improvement in pupil behaviour and teacher-pupil relationships, drawing further upon a hugely influential behaviour management approach whereby expectations and boundaries are exemplified by calm, consistent and regulated adults.

The book delivers a blueprint for school behaviour improvement that is inclusive, practical and well structured – and covers a range of key issues, including: restorative practice, emotionally consistent teaching, creating a coaching culture, and proportionate and productive consequences for bad behaviour.

It also shares indispensable advice about how to involve all staff in developing a whole-school ethos rooted in kindness, empathy and understanding, and features a section for governors on how they can play a part in the school's behaviour policy too.

Suitable for teachers and school leaders – in any setting – who are looking to upgrade their approach to school behaviour.